To Marcia
In appreciation for
modeling strong school
leadership for early educ...
leadership   With best wi...
and thanks,
Catherine

Inside PreK
Classrooms

Inside PreK Classrooms

A School Leader's Guide to Effective Instruction

Judith A. Schickedanz and
Catherine Marchant

HARVARD EDUCATION PRESS
CAMBRIDGE, MASSACHUSETTS

Paperback ISBN 978-1-68253-127-3
Library Edition ISBN 978-1-68253-128-0

Library of Congress Cataloging-in-Publication Data
Names: Schickedanz, Judith A., 1944- author. | Marchant, Catherine, (Writer on education), author.
Title: Inside PreK classrooms : a school leader›s guide to effective instruction / Judith A. Schickedanz and Catherine Marchant.
Description: Cambridge, Massachusetts : Harvard Education Press, 2018. | Includes bibliographical references and index.
Identifiers: LCCN 2017045642| ISBN 9781682531273 (pbk.) | ISBN 9781682531280 (library edition)
Subjects: LCSH: Early childhood education--Curricula--United States--Case studies. | Early childhood education--Activity programs--United States--Case studies. | Classroom management--United States--Case studies. | Play--United States--Case studies. | Language arts (Early childhood)--Curricula--United States--Case studies. | Reading (Early childhood)--Curricula--United States--Case studies.
Classification: LCC LB1139.4 .S34 2018 | DDC 372.210973--dc23
LC record available at https://lccn.loc.gov/2017045642

Published by Harvard Education Press,
an imprint of the Harvard Education Publishing Group

Harvard Education Press
8 Story Street
Cambridge, MA 02138

Cover Design: Wilcox Design
Cover Image: Fat Camera/E+/Getty Images

The typefaces used in this book are Berkeley Oldstyle and Optima LT

CONTENTS

CHAPTER 1

Introduction

THIS BOOK IS FOR INSTRUCTIONAL LEADERS, especially elementary school principals and early childhood directors and content specialists, who want to learn more about preschool-age learners and preK programming and instruction. Ideas about how to educate four-year-olds for later success in school have shifted dramatically over the years and continue to shift as we learn more about how young children learn and about the benefits of preK for long-term academic success and social and emotional outcomes that support it. At the same time, the accountability movement has put enormous pressure on educators to pack as much learning as possible into the preK day to level the playing field for all children. These expectations have sparked many debates among early educators, including how to reconcile developmentally appropriate practice (DAP) with expectations embedded in state early learning standards and preK classroom quality checklists; how to best integrate preK within the elementary school setting; how to manage the preK classroom to maximize child-teacher interaction, and how to design instruction to build literacy and math skills without boring students, to name a few.

To help answer these important questions, we place the reader inside instructional contexts where teacher and child behavior unfolds. We then analyze the situation described and, through this process, make important points and offer suggestions for educators based on our combined experience of more than ninety years in preK classrooms. In other words, we take events and turn them into case studies about some of the most critical topics in preK education.[1] Sometimes our analysis focuses on a specific learning domain, such as oral language or number. At other times, we focus on the design of instruction or the organization of the physical environment. At still other times, a case is concerned with managing child behavior or understanding a specific characteristic of preschoolers' minds.

There are a lot of moving parts inside instructional settings, and small things can make a big difference in how well things go. We focused each case to make situations easier to grasp, while also keeping in mind that instructional situations are complex and that a case loses power if oversimplified. A reader will probably get the gist of a chapter with a fairly quick first reading. Deeper understanding, however, will require a bit of studying in subsequent readings. We suggest that readers consider the book a resource to which they return as needed. For example, when planning for a conference after a classroom observation, a specific chapter might come to mind as especially relevant.

We did not set out to provide a comprehensive overview of preK curriculum and instruction or a complete picture of preschool children as learners. Our goal, instead, was to provide stories to prompt readers to think deeply and in new ways about preK-level teaching and learning. Each chapter's key event is based on our personal experiences in preK classrooms, in the roles of curriculum developer, coach to teachers or district-based mentors, supervisors of beginning teachers, or outside program evaluators. We used pseudonyms for both children and teachers and, on several occasions, combined related events from two or more classrooms into one prototype to allow a more complete treatment of the preschooler's learning or a difficulty that preK teachers experience. The chapters rest more heavily on our experience in programs for lower-income children whose later school achievement is at risk than on our experience with children in more economically secure communities, because these settings are typically more challenging for preK teachers and are where we spent much of our time over the fifteen to twenty years before writing this book.

The book has five parts. The chapters in part I focus on classroom organization and management, especially on how the lack of teacher attention to organization and management hinders children's learning. The three chapters in part II focus on the many contributions that play makes to a preschooler's learning. Part III is concerned with literacy skills and oral language, with two chapters devoted to each topic. The three chapters in part IV are also concerned with some aspect of literacy and oral language, but the specific focus here is on understanding the interactions between preschool children's thinking and their learning. The three chapters in part V consider leadership for preK in elementary school settings, with one devoted to communication between teachers and a building leader, another devoted to a discussion of professional development, and the third to how preK classrooms and teachers were fully integrated into an elementary school setting. Each part has an opening description that provides more details about the key points made in its chapters.

The reader will notice that we have several central concerns about preK education. First is the balance in preK programming between a focus on literacy and numeracy skills and attention given to other domains that preK standards address (e.g., science, social-emotional development, physical development and health, science, social studies, creative arts). Numeracy and language and literacy get most of the attention in many preK programs, and within the areas of language and literacy, literacy skills often get more attention than oral language. Then, within oral language, oral vocabulary often gets more attention than broader language skills, such as listening comprehension and back-and-forth conversations.

Second, we are concerned about both the quantity and quality of teacher-directed, whole-group instruction in some preK programs. Often, academic skills instruction is repetitive and boring, yields knowledge of isolated facts without much understanding, and runs the risk of creating in children negative attitudes toward school and learning. Many instructional approaches used in these contexts squander, rather than exploit, the preschool child's cognitive capacity. An additional problem is that so much time is spent in teacher-directed, whole-group, academic instruction in some classrooms that time for child-selected activities, including play, is squeezed to the minimum. This change is shortsighted, because child-directed activities can support social skills that are essential to academic success (e.g., self-regulation and executive functioning), develop positive attitudes toward learning, and provide opportunities for preschoolers to apply and consolidate learning from other parts of the preK day.

A third concern is that preK teachers sometimes rely too heavily on prepared curricula. Even though core curriculum materials provide essential guidance for novice teachers, they can limit teacher development, especially when supervisors and other leaders require rigid fidelity in the implementation of highly prescriptive curricula. Teachers need to depart from the teachers' guides to adapt materials to their own circumstances. With support and feedback, exercising judgment is at the heart of teacher development.[2]

The remainder of this introduction provides a historical overview of preK education in the United States. Preschoolers are relative newcomers to the public school setting, and the history of preschool education differs from that of the elementary school. An acquaintance with the history of preschool-level education helps instructional leaders in public school settings understand preK teachers a little better.

CHILD DEVELOPMENT: NATURE OR NURTURE?

Preschools, once called nursery schools, started in the United States during the child study movement in the 1920s as part of child study institutes. Having children on-site gave researchers easy access for studies. The Laura Spelman Rockefeller Memorial funded nursery schools in these institutes at several universities.[3] Perhaps the best known was the Yale Clinic of Child Development, directed by Arnold Gesell. Gesell's research involved close observation of all aspects of behavior in young children and linking them to chronological age. The norms established indicated the average or typical age at which specific behaviors were expected to appear.[4]

Until the late 1950s, Gesell and many other child development researchers assumed that changes in development—progress from one developmental milestone to the next—resulted primarily from maturation controlled by an internal timetable dictated by each child's genes. A logical conclusion drawn from this theory of development is that intellectual differences in IQ or achievement in school are predetermined, not influenced by experience. Of course, not everyone held a genetic view of readiness during the 1940s and 50s, and educators who didn't tried to build readiness for reading, for example, in the first months of first grade. By the 1950s, reading readiness programs were used in many kindergartens.[5] Educators adhering to a progressive philosophy of education resisted these narrowly focused readiness programs, arguing that children needed mostly time to mature in a context that provided a broad range of rich experiences. Most preschool education leaders remained strongly aligned with norms and the associated wait-for-maturation approach to readiness, because of their history within the child study movement.

James Hymes, a leading figure in progressive preschool and kindergarten education in the middle of the twentieth century, spoke against the idea of building readiness in *Before the Child Reads*: "Harm is done. Books of drills, books of exercises, books for special 'readiness' practice cost money that could be used elsewhere. They cost time that could be better used elsewhere. Too often they result in bareness and meagerness and in poverty of thinking and feeling and doing. These books usurp the hours that could be given to all the rich and worthwhile activities these children are ready for."[6]

In speaking specifically about reading readiness, Hymes claimed that the biological structures of seeing and hearing, both necessary for learning to read, depend primarily on maturation and growth in the early years: "The reader must have keen eyes, observant and attentive. Those eyes must have grown enough so they can quickly see, when they are taught, that *c* and *e* and *o* are different. That *b* and *d* and *p* are not the same . . . Those eyes must be so developed that the child can know right away, when he is taught: *Ball* and *Tall* do not look alike . . . Hearing is the child's nature . . . He will grow—we do not have to force feed him."[7]

This view of development began to crumble in the 1960s in the face of evidence that intelligence and associated academic knowledge were strongly related to a child's early experience. Joe McVicker Hunt's book *Intelligence and Experience* provided a thorough review of the research on the role of experience in the development of intelligence and a bold statement about the new theory's implications: "It is no longer unreasonable to consider that it might be feasible to govern the encounters that children have with their environments, especially during the early years of their development, to achieve a substantially faster rate of intellectual development and a substantially higher adult level of intellectual capacity."[8]

This new view of intelligence prompted the funding of experimental, early intervention programs in the 1960s to test the idea of IQ as malleable. Most of these programs stressed oral language development and general cognitive and social development, not narrow academic skills development; nor were they highly didactic. Outcome measures always included IQ tests, rarely assessments of specific academic skills.[9] Most programs had positive immediate effects, and some had effects that were long term. These positive results opened the door for funding Head Start in 1964.

DEBATES ABOUT WHAT TO TEACH, AND HOW

Some preschool-level leaders feared that new information about the role of experience in intellectual development and academic achievement would lead to the teaching of literacy and numeracy skills, quickly and directly, outside meaningful contexts, and to a decrease in concern for the whole child. As states developed learning standards for K–12, starting in the early 1990s, and for preschool-age learners soon after, the National Association for the Education of Young Children (NAEYC), closely aligned historically with views that gave maturation a prominent role in development, began to publish position statements on DAP. These statements stressed print-rich environments that helped young children see the usefulness of reading and writing, and spoke out against formal instruction in preK and kindergarten. The position statements also stressed the importance of addressing all areas of development and child-initiated learning.[10]

But as concern about kindergarten readiness in lower-income children increased, some preK programs began to include large- and small-group, literacy-related experiences, especially in response to two influential books, *Beginning to Read*, by Marilyn Adams, and *Preventing Reading Difficulties in Young Children*, by Catherine Snow and colleagues.[11] These books diminished the influence of an earlier book, *Emergent Literacy*, by William Teale and Elizabeth Sulzby, which had provided an approach to literacy that was somewhat compatible with DAP.[12] Over time, changes occurred not only in the balance of goals addressed with preschoolers, tipping it more toward academic skills, but also in instructional approaches.

Following the No Child Left Behind Act of 2001 (NCLB), these changes escalated. The legislation affected kindergarten practices directly, which then trickled down to preschoolers, especially those attending preK classrooms located in elementary schools. Principals concerned about meeting fourth-grade benchmarks had learned that a good start toward building foundational literacy skills in the preschool years could help. How this was accomplished was sometimes more in line with kindergarten practices than with practices that had been more typical in preschools. Early Reading First (ERF) funding was also provided in the NCLB legislation to develop excellent programs to support language, literacy, and cognitive development in preschoolers.[13] ERF grants, awarded by the US Department of Education, required applicants to describe how they would address oral language and three literacy skills—print awareness, phonological awareness, and alphabetic knowledge—in a planned and coherent way. ERF applicants were also required to assess oral vocabulary (receptive), phonological awareness, and alphabetic knowledge, in fall and spring of each year, using standardized tools. Guidance for proposals indicated that programs should provide a variety of different contexts for children's learning, including teacher-directed or teacher-guided large and small groups, in addition to the child-initiated activities that most preschool-level classrooms already provided in a daily Center Time. The prospect of ERF funding also prompted publishers to create instructional materials for the preK level. The National Science Foundation funded the development of math curricula for the preschoolers in the late 1990s, and commercial publishers made those available, too.[14]

PRESCHOOL-LEVEL PROGRAM EFFECTIVENESS

As programs for preschool-age children expanded, research continued to look at their benefits, especially on long-term achievement. The evidence suggested that high-quality experiences for three- and four-year-olds made a significant difference in school readiness and later school achievement and were cost effective, but also that quality was extremely uneven.[15] A 2016 analysis of the effectiveness of ten early intervention programs summed up the findings: "Research shows neither that 'pre-K' works nor that it does not; rather, it shows that some early childhood programs yield particular outcomes, sometimes, for some children."[16]

Results of a statewide preK program in Tennessee, published in 2015, provided a jarring example of an ineffective preK program. At the end of preK, program children's achievement was higher than the achievement of control children on all outcome measures, and the program children's kindergarten teachers said the program children were better prepared for school and had better school-related work skills. By the end of kindergarten, however, the control children's achievement had caught up. Achievement levels were still the same for the two groups at the end of first grade, although first-grade teachers' ratings of program children's work skills and attitudes toward school were more negative than the control children's. By the end of second grade, the control children's academic achievement was better than the program children's, and this situation held through third grade.[17]

UNCERTAINTY ABOUT WHAT MAKES PREK EFFECTIVE

In a Brookings Institution report, Dale Farran, a researcher involved in the Tennessee study, spoke candidly about preK education: "Lack of evidence about which skills and dispositions are most important to effect in pre-K and what instructional practices would affect them has led us to the current situation of poorly defined, enormously varied programs, all called pre-K, as well as a reliance on a set of quality measures with no empirical validity."[18]

The quality measures Farran considered problematic included the Early Childhood Environment Rating Scale Revised (ECERS-R), the Classroom Assessment Scoring System (CLASS), and the benchmark ratings created by the National Institute for Early Education Research (NIEER). According to Farran, "Each . . . has some notable psychometric problems, yet each . . . has been woven into quite consequential policies. None . . . was developed on the basis of empirical knowledge of which skills are most important to affect in pre-K."[19]

In a subsequent Brookings paper, Farran raised concerns about teacher-directed, large-group instruction in preK and questioned whether the trend toward whole-group instruction in kindergarten had made its way into programs for preschoolers. She also worried that increases in preK funding for classrooms in public school settings would turn preK into a beginning level of kindergarten.[20] In our experience, inappropriate and inadequate programming for four-year-olds is not confined to public school settings. Each setting (e.g., Head Start, community-based childcare, public schools) has its own biases and blind spots, and also strengths.

CONCERNS ABOUT PREK EXPANSION

Despite the long-standing issues surrounding preK quality, including unanswered central questions about exactly what a child might learn in preK that matters for long-term academic success, policy makers and politicians currently agree that education for four-year-olds should continue as an approach to decreasing the achievement gap and income inequality, and expand to meet the need.[21] Head Start has never enrolled more than approximately 50 percent of income-eligible children, and the need for early education is greater now than thirty or forty years ago when the achievement gap was between lower-income and middle- and higher-income children, not between lower- and middle-income children and their higher-income peers, as it is today.[22]

Many early educators also want universal education for four-year-olds to replace the targeted funding used historically to serve only very low-income children of preschool age.[23] As many view education for preschool-age children as an important social investment, funding for additional preK classrooms is likely to materialize. The danger is that increases in preK classrooms won't be accompanied by major improvements in the quality of programming provided. That's where instructional leadership can make a difference, and we hope that this book will help.

PART I

Managing the PreK Classroom

Decisions about what preschoolers should learn and be able to do are based on consideration of the age-level mastery items provided in standards. Decisions about how to support preschoolers in learning what standards stipulate are guided by position papers on developmentally appropriate practice, research studies, and tools designed to assess preK classroom quality.[1] Publishers claim that they and their preK curricula authors have distilled all the standards, research, position statements, and quality tools to create organized programs of experience that make the preK teacher's job much easier. But despite all these supports, teachers still must make myriad decisions about how best to use curriculum materials, and they and instructional leaders must constantly consider differing interpretations of research results, accommodate practices to new research findings, and think about how research findings relate to their children's specific circumstances.[2] In short, making good decisions about curriculum and instruction requires teacher judgment, and good implementation requires skill in interacting well with children. These things come only with experience and considerable support along the way.[3]

In a well-organized and well-managed preK classroom, teachers establish a daily schedule and basic routines to help the children function well, and they prevent most behavior problems by balancing young children's capacity to attend to teacher-directed instruction in whole-group and small-group settings with their equally demanding need to move physically, make choices, and learn through play. Teachers in well-managed preK classrooms spend most of their time interacting to support children's learning, not preparing materials, reviewing plans, supervising children, or dealing with misbehavior. Children in well-managed classrooms spend most of their time engaging productively in activities and interacting with peers in mostly considerate ways. That is, children pay attention to the teacher in whole-group and small-group activities, follow basic rules and established routines, treat materials with respect, and work and play appropriately with classmates, though, of course, not without occasional conflicts and disagreements.

Managing a preK classroom is not easy, and many preK classrooms fall far short of providing high-quality experiences for children.[4] Each chapter in part I addresses a problem a teacher experienced in organizing and managing some aspect of a preK classroom. Chapter 2 focuses on a whole-group story-reading setting in which many children disengaged because they had to wait for a long time with nothing to do, while their teacher involved a few children individually in a print-focused activity before starting to read the story. This teacher also did not know effective ways to recapture the children's attention when she was ready to read the story.

Chapter 3 focuses on two management challenges a teacher faced: (1) children's general lack of interest in the writing center, and (2) an unequal distribution of children across centers, which affected their peer relationships negatively and prevented teachers from distributing their time equitably. Chapter 4 also focuses on Center Time and the problems with the physical environment's organization, including the selection of materials in some centers. The demands of physical environment management required so much of the teachers' time that they could not engage meaningfully with children to support their learning.

The setting for chapter 5 is a small-group science activity. Problems arose for a beginning teacher who misjudged the children's readiness to explore materials independently. A revised plan, with a different balance between children's independent action and the teacher's guidance, was implemented successfully the next day. The specific details of the successful revision are contrasted with the original plan to highlight why it worked.

CHAPTER 2

Are you ready?

Organizing Instruction
for Engagement

THE TEACHER HELD UP THE NEW BOOK and pointed to the young boy on its cover: "This is Peter," she said, "and he's walking through the snow. See his footprints?" She pointed to the footprints and then read the title, *The Snowy Day*, while underlining the words with her finger.[1] But instead of opening the book and beginning to read, as she usually did, the teacher said, "I wonder . . . Does anyone see the letter *S* in one of these words? (*She gestures toward the title.*) Raise your hand if you see an *S*." The teacher called on one child who stood to the right of her chair. She turned the book to face him, which cut off the other children's visual access to the title. The child searched for a moment and then pointed to *S*. As he returned to his seat on the floor, the teacher turned the book toward the group, pointed to *S*, and said, "Here's *S*, right here at the beginning of *SNOWY*."

The teacher then asked if anyone saw *D* in a word. The child she called on this time stood in the same place as the previous child, and the teacher oriented the book again for the child's benefit. After the child had located the *D*, the teacher turned the book toward the group and pointed out *D* at the beginning of *DAY*. The teacher selected four more letters, first

T and then *N, W,* and *H,* and chose a child each time to come identify it. After a child found *T* at the beginning of *THE,* the teacher commented that this title was great for finding letters, because all the letters were big and uppercase, and many were also the first in the children's names.

By my count, more than half the children had stopped paying attention by the end of this seven-minute letter lesson. Some children talked quietly to one another, a couple pulled at loose threads sticking out from the edges of their carpet mats, one unbuttoned and buttoned her sweater, and a boy in the back stretched out on the floor. No one was loud or disruptive, but many children had found other things to do while one classmate at a time searched for a letter. To get the children's attention before starting to read the story, the teacher asked, "Are you ready?" Her tone indicated annoyance, not enthusiasm about sharing the book. Apparently, the teacher had expected the children to turn to her immediately when the letter lesson was over.

Several children responded to this prompt, but for those who didn't, the teacher repeated her question, this time adding, "I'm waiting . . . ," in a tone that indicated a bit more annoyance. Two children, who had continued to talk quietly, stopped now and turned their attention to the teacher. But two other children, who had turned to the teacher the first time, turned toward one another this time, and smiled. The girl fiddling with her buttons, who had also looked up in response to the first prompt, turned around, apparently interested in knowing who was not yet paying attention. The teacher called the boy in the back by name and asked him to sit up and look at her and the book, adding, "Everyone is waiting on you." He sat up, and the teacher began to read the story.

The letter lesson and getting children's attention had consumed about ten minutes of the twenty minutes allocated for story time in the daily schedule. Today, it lasted almost thirty minutes, which left no time for the teacher to ask the discussion question she had planned. She asked instead, "Did you like the story?" There was no time for children to respond, and the teacher ended story time by commenting that "Peter had fun in the snow."

MANAGING INSTRUCTION FOR BEHAVIOR AND LEARNING

Earlier in the year, the teacher had not used story time to support print skills. She had started including a print-skills focus during story time only recently, after the reading specialist in the school had shared some research about using this context to increase young children's print knowledge.[2] But always before, the teacher had pointed to the first letters in the words in book titles, and with only two to three words in most titles, letter lessons lasted only a few seconds, hardly long enough for children's attention to stray. Today's approach of asking a child to come up to point to a letter, combined with using more letters, made the letter lesson last much longer, too long for children without any direct engagement in the activity. Spending this much time on letters had also violated the children's expectations for story time. The situation probably puzzled them and made them uneasy.

In addition to not reading the story soon after she had introduced the book, the teacher's focus on one child at a time was not a good instructional approach for a whole-group setting. The teacher did not include the children who were sitting on the floor, as individual children took their turns. Their only involvement was looking as the teacher pointed quickly to the letter after the child chosen had found it. But getting an answer without having searched for the letter did not involve confirmation or violation of any cognitive activity. Without cognitive engagement, a situation is not interesting. Without interest, engagement typically wanes.

The teacher viewed the children's failure to turn their attention to her immediately after the letter lesson as a behavior problem, not as a reasonable reaction to the instructional situation. Had the teacher understood the situation differently, she would have held the book up and said, "Okay, I'm going to read the story now. I wonder what Peter will do in the snow when he goes out to play?" For the few children who might not have engaged with this approach, the teacher probably could have pulled them in soon after starting to read, by saying, "Oh, [child's name]. Do you see what Peter saw when he looked out his window? Look at all that snow! I wonder what Peter does after he gets out of bed on this snowy day?"

INSTRUCTIONAL OPTIONS AND GOALS FOR STORY TIME

When teachers focus on individual children in a whole-group instructional setting, they risk losing the attention of those who are not directly involved. Rather than use the title on the book's cover for this letter lesson, the teacher could have written it on a piece of chart paper before story time and then clipped the paper to a stand. Then, children sitting on the floor could have seen the title as an individual child searched for each letter. The teacher could have asked the other children to search for the letter, too, but to keep thoughts to themselves until the child chosen had pointed it out.

This approach could have solved one problem, but a deeper problem at the curriculum level was at play here, too. When thinking about curriculum, teachers must decide when in the preK day to address each of their many goals for children's learning. When deciding to meet multiple goals in one context, a teacher must then consider how best to organize instruction to accomplish this. Apparently, this teacher, like many preK teachers, thought underlining the words in a book's title was important for developing print skills (e.g., learning the left to right convention and that space separates words in a line of print). This strategy for supporting print skills works well because underlining the title when reading it does not interfere with the goal of reading the title to prompt expectations about the story (i.e., to begin thinking about meaning). In contrast, asking individual children to identify the letters in words in the title is done just for its own sake. The same can be said about pointing to and naming first letters in words in the title, as this teacher had done before. Even though that approach had not caused the children's attention to stray, it surely took their minds away from thinking about the upcoming story. Should we want children to turn their attention immediately to letters in the words of a storybook's title rather than to thinking about the title's meaning in relation to the cover's illustration?

Some early childhood language and literacy researchers have raised the question about the appropriate balance between print-related and meaning-related learning in the book-reading context. One researcher cautioned about focusing on print skills in the book-sharing context because attention to print skills limits the focus on meaning.[3] She also noted that reading development occurs in two phases, learning to read and then reading to learn (i.e., comprehending to get information), and that print skills are strong predictors of decoding or word recognition (i.e., learning to read), while language, content knowledge, and inferential reasoning are strong predictors of later comprehension (i.e., reading to learn).[4] In other words, research indicates that a primary focus on print skills with preschoolers is a benefit when they are learning to read, but print skills, though necessary, are not sufficient for later comprehension.

I (Judy) agree with this caution, especially because advocates of teaching print skills in the book-reading context haven't limited their suggestions to identifying letters in book titles. Among their other suggestions is asking the children on which page the reader should look first after turning to a new page to help children learn that the reader attends to the left page before the right page. After that, the suggestion is for the teacher to ask where to look on the left page to start reading to help children recognize print as distinct from pictures, and to realize that the adult reads the words. Another suggestion is to point to the words, as opposed to a letter, to build a concept of a word in a line of print.[5] Teachers are also advised to choose books with print worked into their illustrations and with portions of the written text in different fonts (e.g., larger and bold-faced).[6]

Might it be better to choose most books based on whether they relate to the content of a current unit of study, expose children to a variety of authors, or use interesting and high-quality language? Advocates of a print focus during book reading also recommend tracking the print as it is read—underlining with a finger. Tracking print can diminish attention to phrasing, intonation, and stress, which help to convey meaning. And when looking at the book mostly to track print, a teacher's facial expressions and body language cannot help to convey meaning. When teachers instead look at the children while reading, they can gauge the children's engagement and interest, and indicate also that they, too, are engaged in the story, wondering or worrying about a character and sharing in some unexpected turn of events.

IMPLICATIONS FOR INSTRUCTIONAL LEADERS

There are often unintended consequences to instructional decisions, which include undermining one goal while addressing another, decreasing children's interest and engagement, increasing behavior problems, and turning experiences, once full of joy and delight, into dull and mind-numbing lessons. As goals for preK and expectations for meeting these have increased, it has become more difficult to decide when and where to address each goal, and increasingly necessary to address multiple goals in a single context. This situation is especially acute in half-day preK programs.

Instructional leaders should discuss instructional organization with preK teachers and provide support, especially when goals are clashing or seem out of balance in context. There may be far too many weary expressions on four-year-olds' faces, and too many teachers with an edge of annoyance in their voices, which suggests that they, too, are weary. Teachers have too little time to think through all the instruction they must now provide and work out what goes where, and when. Instructional leaders might convene a meeting with this as the topic for discussion.

CHAPTER 3

I'd love for you to visit my writing center.

Managing Center Time

I (CATHERINE) OFFERED TO VISIT classrooms in conjunction with the professional development on emergent writing I was providing for the preK teachers in an elementary school. One teacher accepted, saying, "I'd love for you to visit my writing center. I want to improve it." When I arrived, children were putting lunch and recess items away and gathering on the rug. Soon, the teacher sat down and clapped a pattern. After the children clapped back, she started introducing centers:

> In dramatic play, you can continue taking care of the babies and pets. In blocks, you could build cages to set up a zoo for the new animals I put there. At the art easel, you can mix red and blue paint, and see what happens. Of course, books are in the library and puzzles are on the manipulatives table. Something special today is our visitor (*looks at me*). She'll help you add to books if you started one yesterday, and make cards, if you'd like. She's a teacher, too.

As the teacher started asking each child individually to choose a center to start, I left for the writing center to get oriented. A tray on the table held both unfinished books and materials for making more blank books, but not any card-making materials. I also didn't see a basket or tray with card supplies on the nearby shelves. I did see scissors, paper in varied sizes, and writing and drawing tools, all of which could be used for making cards, but I knew that I would need to assist children in gathering the items.

Two girls soon arrived. One found her unfinished book on the tray, told me it was her animals book, and then read its cover, "*Animals*, by Loresha." Then, she opened the book and "read" three finished pages (e.g., "Here is a cat. Here is a dog. This is a bird."). The first two words on the cover were computer-generated print; Loresha had written her own name on a printed line that extended beyond "by." Anyone just listening to Loresha read the pages would not have known that each page had only a picture, no words.

The second girl selected a blank book, wrote her name on its cover, and announced that this new book was going to be about flowers, "because me and my Mom plant flowers." Although she asked me to write "flowers" on the cover, I explained instead how I could help: "If we say, 'flowers,' slowly, and listen for the sounds, we can spell it together." She rejected the offer, saying, "No, thanks. I'll just put a flower on here." After she finished drawing, I commented that a flower picture is a good clue that her book's title is *Flowers*, but adding the word would let people know for sure. "I know that," she said, but did not add *Flowers*.

For preK children, both drawing and talking are important for communicating their messages when at the writing table.[1] But children of preschool age start using print, too, especially in books, even if wavy-line scribbles they interpret. I was thinking about ways to encourage the girls' interest in print when loud arguing over a toy lion in the block area interrupted. As the two boys' voices escalated, the girls stopped to stare. Although the dispute ended quickly with help from the teacher, the girls reengaged only half-heartedly with their books. Within a few minutes, they left the writing center and headed to the art easel. I noticed that other children were also leaving their first centers to find another one.

When no one else came to the writing center over the next five to ten minutes, I invited two boys who were standing nearby. They declined.

There were now no children in the writing center, the library, or the puzzles and manipulatives area. In contrast, the dramatic play area was very crowded. I asked the boys, still standing nearby, how children know whether they may join a center. "You just go and get in," one said. I asked next about rules for how many children may play in a center at one time. The boys agreed: "You just go in if you want to." Then I asked how children got materials, once in a center. The boys' responses boiled down to this: "You just take things." Another outburst erupted in the blocks and interrupted our conversation. The teacher was now insisting that a boy return cars brought from home to his cubby. She had explained to him earlier that toys from home were only for the afterschool program, but he had taken them to the block area anyway to roll down a ramp.

Typically, twenty to twenty-five minutes into Center Time, most preschoolers are deeply engaged. But in this classroom, children moved quickly from center to center as more time passed. After the teacher announced cleanup time, the children returned items to shelves and cabinets, hurriedly and without much care. When finished, they dashed to the rug for the goodbye routine. Walking is typically the rule in a preK classroom.

THE DEBRIEF

After the children had left, the teacher started our conversation by saying that afternoon centers had been difficult, much worse than the morning's, and that the behavior of the child prone to outbursts was now affecting everyone. She then refocused quickly by saying, "But you are here to help me with the writing center. What did you notice, and how can I make it better?" After acknowledging the difficult afternoon, I commented about the two girls' disinterest in print. The teacher indicated that expecting preschool children to use print along with their drawings was new to her. Though experienced, she had only just moved to this public elementary school and was still learning about expectations in this context. She added that she needed all the help she could get and revealed that this was her motivation for accepting my offer to visit classrooms. Then she asked for suggestions:

To increase children's interest in print, I explained how she could describe materials and possibilities for their use in the various centers more fully, when introducing children to Center Time, which she did daily. I related what the teacher had said today and then how she might expand it:

> Today, you told children they could finish books already started or make cards. The tray on the table held books in process and materials for making more blank books, but not card-making materials. I saw appropriate materials on the shelves, but without knowing they must gather card-making materials, children might not have known how to get started. You can also show items when talking about a center to spark interest and provide ideas to help children engage, once in the center. This supports self-regulation, too, because children have more cognitive resources to bring to their experiences.[2] Today, you might have shown a couple of unfinished books, a new blank book, and a piece of paper folded for a card. Mentioning some card uses might also help, for example, for someone's birthday or to welcome a classmate back to school following an absence.

I also suggested showing one item again when she called children to each center, to remind them what was there, and choosing only a specific number of children for each center, not everyone who raised a hand. This would prevent overcrowding, at least at the start. The teacher liked these ideas, but worried that including details and showing items would make Introduction to Centers too long. After some discussion, the teacher agreed that the time saved by calling the centers, not each child individually, would allow her to provide more information about the centers.

Next, we discussed the current picture-related resources at the writing center (e.g., wordless picture books, a how-to-draw book, picture charts) and some print resources she might add: sets of children's name tags, card-related words (e.g., DEAR, MOM, DAD, LOVE), small alphabet charts, and a picture dictionary. From there, we discussed writing in other centers, during Center Time, and at other times in the preK day. For example, in the block center, showing a book with images of zoo animals and their names on cages or fences might inspire children to make signs, especially if a teacher demonstrates quickly with a clipboard, marker, and a strip of card-weight paper, and tells children the supplies are in the block area. For dramatic play, role-playing how to check items on a picture and word list of baby- and pet-food items to make a shopping list might inspire children to do the same before leaving on a pretend trip to a store.

When we turned to writing at other times of the day, we considered Circle Time. For example, a teacher and children could compose a thank-you note to a janitor or an invitation to both the janitor and the principal to come view the children's paintings displayed in the hall. The teacher could start by discussing with the children what the note should say and then, when writing, explain that a note begins with "Dear," that "Dear" starts with /d/, and we spell /d/ with *D*. I provided information about spelling comments when the teacher asked for additional details:

> It's too time consuming and tedious to belabor every word's spelling or even all sounds in a word. Just provide a hint here and there about first sounds and their spellings. You can do more, gradually, as children have more experience with this. From these experiences, children will develop some knowledge and skill that could increase their acceptance of a teacher's offer to help spell words at the writing table. If the message is placed in the upper portion of the chart paper, children who want to can sign their names underneath during Center Time.

We scheduled another visit in two weeks to discuss the teacher's implementation of as many suggestions as made sense and time allowed. I also promised to drop off resources about preschoolers' writing, with a second set for the principal.[3]

THE SECOND VISIT

At the beginning of Introduction to Centers, the teacher stated that I would help in all the centers, not just in the writing center. Then she lifted a bin to her lap and started introducing the centers:

> There are many interesting things in today's centers. Listen carefully, because I will ask you to choose one center after telling you about all of them. Yesterday, in the *blocks*, some of you made tanks for the fish and icebergs for the penguins (*shows a picture*). Today, we have an aquarium worker to feed the fish and penguins, tiny pails for pretend food (*shows*), a diver, and a person with boots and a bucket. We have only two of each prop, but I know you will share. In *dramatic play*, pictures of our aquarium visit are now on the walls. You can show these to your babies and talk about the fish and penguins. (*Walks a few steps to the center; demonstrates talking to a doll about penguins in one picture.*) Then, you can dress the babies and take them on a trip to the pretend aquarium in the blocks.

The teacher showed books about aquariums, seal animals, and marine biologists, and walked to the *library area* to leave them there. On the way, she explained that marine biologists are people who work in an aquarium. On the way back, she said, "I think I'll see a lot of readers today." Then, she described the remaining centers:

> In the *writing center*, you can borrow library books to find words to label your aquarium drawings. Or, you may use new word cards. "Miss T. [assistant teacher], you could label the tank and shark in the aquarium picture you drew yesterday, using the new aquarium word cards. Here's 'tank' (*holds up; reads*)."

Miss T. said she liked the word cards and asked about "penguin." "It's in the set at the writing table," the teacher explained. Then the teacher told about the webcam at the *computer*: "Just press the triangle (*pointed to on a still photo*) to watch the fish swim by."

Before calling the centers, the teacher told the children to indicate their interest by raising a hand and to remember that they could choose another center if their first choice did not have enough space. She called the block area first and chose four children from among the six raised hands. She quickly assured the children not chosen that they could move to the blocks during Center Time, "when space opens up." She offered the other centers in the same way, except for the computer. The teacher delayed talking about it because Introduction to Centers had already lasted more than twenty minutes, far past the intended fifteen. The teacher asked two boys who had not yet chosen a center to stay on the rug for a moment while she helped children settle in at their chosen centers. Upon her return, she explained that she hadn't viewed all of the ocean tank webcam photos and wondered whether the boys could help her. They said they could.

As Center Time began, the children were engaged. The room was busy in a good way. I hoped the engagement and calm atmosphere would continue after children finished in their first center and looked for another. In about twenty minutes, I realized that problems remained. Several children had moved to the dramatic play area about ten minutes earlier, which had caused a severe shortage of doll clothes. The teacher left the computer area to search for more clothes and then stayed to help children dress the dolls. By the time all the dolls were dressed, the children were eager to take a pretend trip to the play aquarium in the block area. The teacher stayed to guide them, given the current crowded conditions there.

The two boys who had been at the computer had moved to the blocks soon after the teacher had headed to dramatic play. They joined the four children who had started there, and one of them soon grabbed a prop that a girl had been playing with. She protested loudly: "Hey, don't touch that! We put icebergs together for the penguins to jump on!" In response, Miss T. moved from the writing center to help the two boys find enough space and props to join the aquarium play. She stayed, sensing that more conflicts were likely in the offing, given the crowding. The children aban-doned at the writing center had disengaged from their activities to watch Miss T. help resolve the dispute. After realizing that she would not return, they left the writing center.

At this point, most of the children who had started in the writing cen-ter or the library area had moved to the block and dramatic play areas. At three centers (writing, puzzles/manipulatives, and library), there were no children; a single child was at the computer, and two or three children were wandering. Noise and conflicts increased, despite teachers' frequent pleas "to remember to share." The teacher signaled cleanup earlier than usual. As children gathered on the rug, she told them she was concerned that they hadn't been able to share materials and play together. She ended the morning by reading *It's Mine*.[4] This book choice suggested that other mornings had probably been a lot like this one.

THE DEBRIEF

The teacher expressed disappointment about the disintegration of Cen-ter Time, but quickly noted that changes since the first visit produced positive effects overall. She said that she now showed items and used role-playing in Introduction to Centers. She had added resources to the writing center and other centers, and had done a few writing demonstra-tions over the past two weeks at Circle Time. She thought the children were more enthusiastic about the centers and much better at making a first choice. She had also seen more print on drawings and cards, and more messages going home. Overall, she had seen very positive results.

I agreed, and listed more changes and positive results: "The children were very attentive during Introduction to Centers and engaged produc-tively in their first center choice. In the writing center, children wrote their names on drawings and often labeled objects in pictures, with a teacher's help." Before I could say more, the teacher jumped in: "But it never lasts! Once children start moving, the movers disrupt children already in the centers they enter, and everyone gets louder and more rambunctious, as the arguments start about toys." I said, "Okay. Let's focus first on why the centers started out well today, and then why things fell apart. After that, we can discuss changes that might help sustain productive play for the duration of Center Time."

The teacher agreed to the plan, and I gave my analysis:

Introduction to Centers provided ideas about what children could do in each center, and materials added to the centers supported the children's engagement. At the writing center, the books and name and word cards were organized well (e.g., cups for pencils and markers, trays for paper, a bin for children's work), which helped children find what they needed and put things away. Most importantly, though, you chose a limited number of children for each center, which prevented crowding at the beginning. Overcrowding started because limits had not been established for dramatic play and block centers. These areas soon became crowded, and that's when arguing over materials and space began, just as researchers have documented.[5] When the doll clothes ran out, you left the computer to find more. Then, the boys at the computer moved to blocks. Miss T. left children at the writing center when a girl in the blocks protested about one of the boys taking an aquarium play item she'd been using. Both you and Miss T. stayed in these two crowded areas, which meant that neither of you was available to support the other children. Not surprisingly, Center Time just fell apart. If limits had been established for the children allowed in blocks and dramatic play, I don't think this would have happened.

The teacher explained that she wanted to support children's independent decision making and problem solving, and believed that too many rules stifle preK children's independence and creativity. This statement about social goals for the children and her belief about the effect of rules on these goals led to a long back-and-forth discussion. I argued that limits would not undermine these goals:

Center Time is a complex situation, given its simultaneous activities and the children's freedom to move from one center to another. Research indicates that explaining and demonstrating the centers' activities to the whole group, as you now do, increases children's engagement because they get ideas about what they can do with the materials.[6] Other research indicates that adult interactions with the children during Center Time help sustain their engagement.[7] Without limits in the areas, you and Miss T. were unable to provide support across all the centers because you stayed in crowded areas to deal with behavior issues. Limits in the areas help to ensure that children have sufficient space and materials to implement ideas, decrease negative child-child interactions, and allow teachers to distribute their time among all children.

The teacher indicated that listing children's turns and limiting access to centers bothered her because they decreased children's choices. Center Time was the child-initiated part of the day, and she believed that children should be able to make choices about where to play. Again, I argued that limits and lists of turns would increase choice:

Once in a center, access to more space and materials gives children more choice in implementing their ideas. Turns lists can also help children develop a broader range of interests. While, for a short time, children certainly feel that their choices have been curtailed because they must wait for a turn in a favorite center, their choices often increase over time as they find that some centers they hadn't even considered before are interesting. Choices are also increased for timid children who had been deterred by high noise levels and quarreling in crowded centers. The children who have learned consideration for others at home also often stay away from crowded centers where children grab items, because violating rules at school bothers them. With limits in centers and turns lists, these children now have more choices. Moreover, as teachers distribute their time and attention more equitably, children have more choices of what to do in a center, because they get needed support. All in all, choices increase. Child engagement increases, and this supports both self-regulation and learning.[8]

The teacher was now willing to try limits. We talked briefly about keeping Introduction to Centers to fifteen minutes by focusing mostly on the centers with new items for their use and showing an item quickly for other centers to remind children what was there. I also urged consistency with the new routines, indicating that, at first, some children might fall back on old habits when confronted with a long wait. We discussed how both self-regulation and flexibility in occupying oneself while waiting varies considerably among preschoolers, and that children with lower levels benefit the most from established classroom routines.

IMPLICATIONS FOR INSTRUCTIONAL LEADERS

Every instructional leader responsible for preK teachers needs to know that classroom management, including the use of established routines, supports the development of critical social behavior, which then affects learning not only in preschool, but long after.[9] They must know, too, that child-directed activities also provide opportunities for young children to learn to regulate their behavior.[10] Centers are now more numerous and complex than thirty years ago, when no writing center, literacy and numeracy items in the puzzles and manipulatives area, or print props in block and dramatic play areas were required. This complexity requires even more management skill. Moreover, before academic skill learning was included in preK programming, the education and training of preK teachers emphasized the physical environment and effective strategies for guiding the young child's behavior. Preparation programs no longer spend much time on these matters, especially programs that lead to state licensure, which often span preK through second grade.

These conditions place the burden for classroom management on instructional leaders, who must find resources to support preK teachers in this area. The principal in this school was responsive to the teacher's needs, although she had misjudged the severity of the teacher's Center Time management problems. We collaborated closely as I supported this teacher. The reader can learn about that part of this case in chapter 17, where it is described within a larger discussion about planning for school-wide professional development.

CHAPTER 4

Please hold your funnels over the table.

Designing the Physical Environment

AFTER WORKING FOR ABOUT TWENTY MINUTES to fill her easel paper with colorful shapes, Tamira called to the teacher at the nearby water table to come look. The teacher assured the children that she would be right back. She approached the easel, glanced at Tamira's painting, and commented, "Oh, that's fantastic! Wow! Such great colors! It's just beautiful. Now, please put your name on your painting and hang it on the rack to dry." Immediately after returning to the water table, the teacher asked the children to stop bumping the table, explaining that it caused water to spill onto the floor. Then she put sections of newspaper over the puddles, explaining, "It's getting slippery. I don't want someone to fall." When finished, she said, "Okay, Jabari, you've had that funnel long enough. It's Leila's turn." Managing the water table left no time for this teacher to engage meaningfully with Tamira at the easel or with children in other centers.

This chapter focuses on the effects of a classroom's physical design on teachers' behavior. The discussion starts with more information about the Center Time duties of the two teachers in this classroom and then addresses changes in the physical environment that would have allowed the teachers to spend less time managing the physical environment and supervising children, and more time engaging in quality interactions with them to support their learning.

TWO TEACHERS' CENTER TIME DUTIES

The two teachers in this classroom divided responsibilities for their group of twenty children during Center Time. For the current week, one covered the water table and the art area, which included the easel and a table project, and kept an eye on the center with puzzles, and math and literacy skills materials. The second teacher covered the writing center and the dramatic play and block areas, all on the other side of the room. She, too, watched over the center with puzzles and other materials. Both teachers visually supervised the book center, located between the writing center and the puzzles area. The computer center was used this week only for the twenty-minute, early-morning arrival period, not during Center Time.

The Water Table

With the table two-thirds full, only a little bumping caused waves to splash over its sides. Jabari and Alyssa had difficulty not bumping into it because their funnels were on the ends of the same piece of plastic tubing, which unfortunately was a bit shorter than the table's width. In addition to leaning into the table, the children pulled the funnels toward their bodies to fill them and sometimes failed to aim them squarely over the table when dumping them out. A scarcity of materials at the water table was also a problem, the one that had caused the teacher to monitor turns for a funnel.

Four children could play at the water table at one time, two on each side. The materials the teachers had put there this week included four pieces of plastic tubing with a funnel attached to one end and four dippers. The teacher's idea was that each child would have a funnel and tubing apparatus, and a dipper to fill the funnel. Young three-year-olds would engage with these materials, at least for a while, because they enjoy water play mostly as a sensory experience and as an opportunity for parallel play with peers (i.e., doing the same thing while in one another's company). In contrast, four-year-olds prefer to collaborate with peers and design various uses for materials provided at a water table. Of course, four-year-olds enjoy the water, but not just feeling it. They seek more cognitive challenge than is characteristic of three-year-olds. Their interest is in what they can do with it, using the materials provided. Researchers now help teachers view water tables as a context for substantial science-related learning, and this information is helpful when planning activities for four-year-olds. Some early childhood teachers continue to underestimate the cognitive capacity of older preschoolers and their interest in designing different uses for water table materials and then experimenting to see what happens.[1]

The funnel shortage started when Jabari removed his from its piece of tubing and attached it to the available end of Alyssa's. When Stephen, the third child at the table, noticed the new funnel arrangement, he removed the funnel from the fourth piece of tubing that was floating in the water and placed it on the other end of his. When Leila joined the table, she found two pieces of tubing, but no funnels. She asked for a funnel, but learned that the classroom had only these four. The teacher told her that Alyssa, Jabari, and Stephen had been using two funnels for just a little while and had not finished experimenting. To bide her time while waiting, Leila slapped the tubing pieces gently against the water, dipped water into the end of one, then submerged a piece, watching as bubbles emerged. Before long, the teacher told Jabari it was Leila's turn. After giving his funnel to her, he left for another center.

Some solutions. Solving the problem of water on the floor is easy. A large water table should never be filled more than halfway. With an appropriate amount of water, bumps cause much smaller waves that rarely go over the table's sides. Another solution is to use plastic dishpan tubs, one at each end. Water that sloshes over the tubs' sides falls into the water table, not onto the floor. Though not always suitable, such as when children blow air through a straw onto a sailboat's sails to make it move or want their aquatic animals to go for a swim, tubs are useful for many other situations and help keep water off the floor.

Some preK teachers have solved the water overflow problem by changing from a large water table to a smaller one that accommodates only two children. Or they use a large table that is permanently divided into two separate tubs. Both options solve the problem of overflowing waves, but their designs also limit water play options. Sailboats can move only a little in small spaces, and in a child's mind, a whale needs more room to swim. A large and open water table meets a full range of uses in a preschool classroom, and removable tubs can be set inside for some activities.

Solving the materials shortage requires thinking about appropriate learning goals for four-year-olds and some consideration of their social preferences and skills. They like to explore a wide range of materials and processes, such as the effects of a stream versus a spray on a waterwheel; how different kinds of bottles react in water when empty, partially full, or completely full; or how different kinds of pumps work. Both variety and quantity are important considerations when selecting water table materials for four-year-olds. When planning for a water table, it's worth thinking about the options for play that a collection of materials provides.

The options for the original materials provided in this classroom for the week were very limited. The children could dip water into the funnels and watch it run through the clear plastic tubing, or dip water and just dump it back into the table, perhaps varying the height to see the effect. Children could also slap the water with the tubing to create a splash or pour water through a detached funnel or directly into the tubing from their dipper, as Leila attempted. They could submerge the tubing and watch bubbles emerge, as Leila also tried. Although the materials allowed several options, none was very interesting to the four-year-olds; the teacher's decision to attach a funnel to each piece of tubing and to provide four identical sets also limited what the children did with individual items. Although Leila created options, she probably would not have stayed at the water table, had she not been waiting for a funnel. Jabari's departure after giving his funnel to Leila was not surprising when there was so little there for the children to do.

Other options would be available if ten to twelve plastic bottles, varying in both size and the width of their mouths, were added to the four dippers, funnels, and pieces of plastic tubing. Children could dip water directly into the bottles or place a funnel in the bottles to fill them. If a funnel were attached to a piece of plastic tubing, a child could fill a bottle that way, too, or simply let the water run out into the water table. A child cannot easily hold a bottle and steady the funnel and plastic tubing apparatus, while also dipping water into the funnel, and cannot set the bottles in the water table because empty bottles float. One child could hold a bottle while another filled it. Or a child could submerge some bottles to fill them enough to make them sit up and then finish filling the bottles using a funnel and plastic tube apparatus. The point is, just adding plastic bottles increases children's play options. But their addition would probably not make the water table interesting enough for some four-year-olds, especially those who want to visit that center several times during the week.

If a variety of dippers and funnels were also added, along with a few more pieces of plastic tubing that vary in both diameter and length, the children would have more options. As it turned out, more funnels of three different sizes were available in a storage box. The teacher had said there were only the four in use, because they were the only ones that fit snugly into the pieces of plastic tubing. The children could have put the stored funnels to good use with a variety of bottles. With additional plastic tubing, varying in diameter, the children would have figured out how to match funnels to plastic tubing pieces and bottles. Items provided individually also require assembly, and four-year-olds enjoy thinking about the possibilities and paying attention to specific features of items to make their ideas work. The problem solving—the engineering—engages children deeply, contributes to their learning, and prompts collaboration.

Even a different organization of the table, using tubs to hold the water and placing materials in between them on the bottom of it, would create some interesting possibilities. Two children could share a tub; four could share bottles, funnels, dippers, and tubing. They could use a long piece of tubing to send water from tub to tub, reversing the output and input ends when one tub's water ran low and the other began to overflow. A piece of tubing long enough to coil into several loose loops could be especially interesting as water flows through it, even more so if a very dilute mixture of food coloring, provided in small squeeze bottles, is sent through the funnel into the tubing.

Children could also attach a funnel to one end of a shorter piece of tubing and make a loop near the funnel end, securing it with a plastic clip. The teacher could demonstrate how to make a loop during Introduction to Centers, and the children could experiment with the size of the coil and its placement, such as near the funnel versus farther down, to see how each position works. The children would also probably collaborate, because two pairs of hands are usually needed to secure a coil with a clip.

This collection is just one example of materials that would give four-year-olds enough to experiment with. From week to week, teachers could provide other collections of materials, perhaps a variety of pumps, waterwheels, and boats, or bubble solution with eggbeaters, whisks, and straws. The main considerations are whether the materials lend themselves to various uses, and whether there are enough to accommodate four children productively. Teachers need not provide four of each kind of item, but a variety of interesting items. As the children try different things, each child usually has an opportunity to use each one.

The Writing Center and Block Area

The second teacher started Center Time in the writing center. There was a need for more blank books, because only one remained in the supply basket and all three children who chose the writing table wanted one. The teacher started to make the books quickly for the two children in need, but changed her plan when they begged to help. With the new plan, the teacher helped one child at a time make a blank book. When the first child folded a sheet of paper, making the crease more diagonal than vertical, the teacher provided hand-over-hand assistance. After folding three sheets of paper properly and assembling them to make the book's pages, the teacher positioned a stapler in four places along the folded side while the child helped push it down. After the stapling, the teacher helped the child open each page and press it back against the line of staples, explaining that this would make the pages stay open better when the child later drew or wrote in the book.

Before assisting the second child, the teacher explained that she must visit the block area for a few minutes. Once there, she reminded the children to build their road farther away from the shelves:

> If you build that close to the shelves, Brianna and Jeremy, you can't get to the blocks. You know what happens, right? Uh-huh, someone accidentally bumps into your building and knocks it over, and you're unhappy. Look down here, Brianna. Buildings need to stay on the other side of my foot. Okay? I think we've discussed this before. Please try to remember. We don't want a catastrophe.

After returning to the writing table and helping the second child make a blank book, the teacher quickly assembled three more for the supply basket. Then she made another trip to the block area, staying this time to help move some of the blocks placed too close to the shelves, "our roads," Brianna and Jeremy offered in complaint. "Well," the teacher explained, "the ambulance and police car can't come in on this back road because it's too close to the block shelves." She pointed toward the house the children had built earlier: "Let's move your road to the other side of your house. I'll help you get started." She picked up a few blocks and carried them to the new area.

As the teacher walked back to the writing center, she noticed two mostly empty puzzle frames on the table. A classroom rule stipulated that children should put the pieces back into their puzzle frames, even if not assembled, and return the puzzles to the shelf. This rule helped keep the small table available to other children who might visit and facilitated the official cleanup at the end of Center Time. The teacher remembered who had occupied this center as Center Time had started, but rather than ask those children to leave their current activity, she tidied the puzzles up herself. When she returned to the writing center, she positioned her chair for a good view of the block area. Two children had joined Brianna and Jeremy. All four were playing with vehicles on the road that Brianna and Jeremy had built earlier, but the teacher had overheard some talk about the need for a hospital and maybe a fire station. If those plans materialized, she would probably need to advise again against building too close to the shelves.

The child who had used the last blank book in the supply basket was now finished drawing a food item on most of the book's pages—raisins, cheese sticks, goldfish crackers, and doughnut holes. She first asked the teacher to guess each food depicted. Then she closed the book to expose its cover and asked, "How do you spell 'Star Market'?" The teacher helped by sounding out the words, linking letters to the sounds, and advising about letters needed, though not linked to any sound heard when saying the words (i.e., *a* before /r/). The child then asked for help in spelling the names of the food items. The teacher offered to make a list for the child to copy, explaining that the other children might soon finish their books and ask for help with their titles. She also informed the child that Grandma Rogers, a school volunteer, was scheduled for their classroom in the afternoon. If the child could wait, the teacher would ask Grandma Rogers to help at the writing center. "Besides," she added, "there isn't much time left now for morning centers."

Solving the problems. The decision to help children with their books kept this teacher from monitoring the puzzles area and moving there for a few moments to offer instructional support in assembling puzzles, or to at least remind children to return unfinished puzzles to the shelf. The old proverb "An ounce of prevention is worth a pound of cure" certainly applies here. The best course of action would have been to check the supplies of books for the next day before leaving for the day and replenish them, if needed, before the children arrived the next day. The wiser course of action, in consideration of the other children in the class, would have been to make the needed books quickly and explain why the children's requests to help could not be honored this time.

A preschool-age child's tendency to build too close to the block shelves diminishes when teachers place a physical marker on the floor indicating where children should and should not build. The teacher could use masking tape to draw lines or position the block area rug a foot or so away from the shelves, with the bare floor between it and the block shelves designating the do-not-build zone. The teacher must point out the marker and explain its use; if consistently enforced for a few weeks, honoring the boundaries becomes the norm. With this problem prevented, a teacher could talk with children about their buildings in ways that extend their play. For example, this teacher might have asked on her visits, "Did you call the ambulance and police car to your house, or are they going to a hospital?" If heading to a hospital, the teacher might ask, "Will you pretend there's a hospital farther down the road or do you plan to build one?"

IMPLICATIONS FOR INSTRUCTIONAL LEADERS

When considering professional development for preK teachers, instructional leaders sometimes prefer a focus squarely on content information and instructional strategies for supporting academic content and skills development. But if teachers spend most of their time managing the physical environment and supervising children, they cannot support academic learning or cognitive and social development to the extent they should. It is often wise to arrange for professional development that deals with both classroom organization and management, and goals for learning, rather than primarily the latter, and leaving classroom organization and management to the individual teacher. Chapter 3 provides a good example of what sometimes happens.

When they observe individual teachers, instructional leaders should note whether supervision and other management demands dominate and discuss changes that could free up more of the teacher's time for quality interactions with children. Teachers sometimes make few changes in the physical environment because they don't fully appreciate the importance of quality adult interactions to children's learning. Instructional leaders must work on both fronts. (Chapter 11 describes what might have occurred had the teacher spent some time talking with Tamira about her painting and choices for mixing colors.) Sometimes, an instructional leader might take detailed notes about what one or two children are doing that a teacher is missing and then discuss what might have happened had the teacher spent time with the children. Classroom quality measurement tools are also sometimes helpful. One tool, the Classroom Assessment Scoring System (CLASS), devotes a section specifically to classroom organization, including behavior management, children's productivity, and how well a teacher engages children in learning, which is often related to the quality of the teacher's interactions with the children.[2]

CHAPTER 5

They can't do this. They just aren't ready.

Supporting Self-Regulation

THE FIRST-YEAR TEACHER'S THOUGHTS after attempting to implement a small-group science activity were, "They can't do this. They're just not ready. I'm not doing this with my other groups. They're not interested and would rather play." The activity had gone awry with her first small group and probably would again with the remaining groups slated to take turns over the next two days.

Observing this activity reminded me (Judy) of the time I allowed preschoolers to transfer finger paint from jars to their paper. Some took enough to lather their hands. When it dried, they wanted me to remove it. While supervising the sink, I couldn't monitor the table. In the end, paint was on chairs, smocks, paint jars, dipping spoons, and faucets. Although I declared I would never use finger paint again, a supervisor insisted that I try, but offered this advice: "Don't allow the children to help themselves to the finger paint." The change produced a different result, from which I learned two things: (1) current circumstances dramatically affect preschoolers' behavior, and (2) for each experience, a teacher must determine which materials the children should control and which the teacher should keep under control. An inappropriate balance in the control of materials contributed significantly to the difficulties the teacher experienced in the small group science activity.

This chapter provides details about what happened during the implementation of both the original plan and a revision. I discuss the key differences between the two to identify the likely reasons for one's failure and the other's success.

ORIGINAL PLAN: "MATERIALS THAT ABSORB WATER, AND MATERIALS THAT DON'T"

The science activity had three goals: (1) prompt children to explore materials and observe what happens; (2) increase children's awareness of absorbent and nonabsorbent materials; and (3) build children's knowledge of the materials' properties. The experience was designed for five or six children. In this class, the teacher met with a small group in a separate room, three days a week, while the remaining children participated in Center Time with an assistant teacher. When finished, children from the small group joined Center Time for its final half hour. During three days, all the children participated in the week's small-group activity.

The teacher introduced basic concepts and key vocabulary in a fifteen-minute, whole-group session the day before the first small group met. She sprayed water on an open umbrella as the children observed the droplets run off into the baking sheet on her lap. Children also observed that no droplets formed when the teacher sprayed water on a terry cloth towel placed on one side of the umbrella. The teacher commented that the umbrella's fabric repelled water, while terry cloth absorbed it. The children also saw and discussed water sprayed on a bath towel, a shower cap, and a plastic poncho. At the end of this whole-group session, the children were enthusiastic that they would soon have the opportunity in a small group to test materials with water and observe what would happen.

Materials for testing included construction, waxed, and finger paint paper; corrugated cardboard and aluminum foil; paper toweling, terry cloth, and lamination film; felt-backed vinyl and plastic chips; plastic and metal food container lids; and small wooden blocks. The teacher placed a full array of items, arranged on a large tray, at each end of a table. Small plastic trays, each with an eyedropper and a small bowl of water, defined each child's workstation. Two boxes for collecting the tested items sat on the table near the teacher, one labeled ABSORBENT, the other NOT-ABSORBENT.

Small-Group Implementation

After quickly reminding the children about the previous day's session, the teacher explained that each child would have a workstation with an eyedropper and a dish of water from which to fill it. (The teacher used a workstation at her place to show all items.) The children would select one item at a time from the tray at their end of the table, put it on their workstation tray, and test it with drops of water from their eyedropper. After testing an item, a child was to talk with the teacher about what happened and then place the item in the appropriate collection box. The child would then select another item from the tray to test in the same way, continuing until he or she had tested most of the items offered on the supply tray.

After placing a workstation in front of each child, the teacher told the children to begin. The first problem was that children could not work the eyedroppers. When the teacher advised squeezing the bulb "to force air out" and then "letting go to allow water in," children seemed to understand that they should drop the eyedropper after squeezing its bulb. Some children dipped their eyedropper's tip into the bowl, as if they thought water would travel of its own accord. The teacher's quick demonstration for a child or two didn't help. Before long, the children abandoned the eyedroppers and dumped water into the trays. Soon they added items that they grabbed from the supply trays. One child pretended to wash dishes, while another made "magic soup." Two children held onto the ends of their trays and tipped them first one way and then the other, squealing with delight when contents spilled onto the table. The teacher called for cleanup and collected the children's trays and soggy items. The children and I mopped the table with paper towels I had grabbed from a nearby dispenser.

What went wrong? Although the plan had worked before in other set-tings, there were several reasons for the vastly different outcome this time. The children's behavior was significantly more challenging, the teacher much less experienced, the school more limited in coaching and teacher-to-teacher support, and the plan's instructional guidance a poor match for these circumstances. I suggested revising the plan, rather than aban-doning it. The teacher was wary, and with a second group scheduled to participate the next day, we had no time to revise together. I volunteered to work on the plan that night and implement it the next day, while the teacher observed, because she also had no time early the next morning to familiarize herself with the changes. The teacher agreed.

Back to the drawing board. I added two social-emotional goals: (1) help the children feel competent from the beginning, and (2) support them in regulating their behavior. I selected only some materials from the long list in the original plan and eliminated the eyedroppers, replacing them with small plastic twist-top bottles prefilled with water. The bot-tles eliminated the need for the small dishes of water. I added practice with the bottles' twist tops to the plan and decided to give the children materials, as needed, instead of having them select materials from a large supply tray. We would discuss and judge the property of each item after the children had observed the fate of water drops in my demonstrations, and again after they had tested the same items. I saw no need to quiz the children further using the collection boxes, and without them, I could also move more quickly to the next demonstration after the children had finished testing an item.

I considered the children's prior experience with adult engagement in their learning. Adult-mediated experiences give young children access to "other people's knowledge, imaginative creations, and counterfactual speculation" and treat children as partners in learning about the world.[1] This kind of experience varies considerably, with children from very low-income families typically having fewer experiences than children from more economically secure families.[2] Two days earlier, the children had responded well to the teacher's whole-group demonstrations. They needed an opportunity to test items and also a playful and concrete approach, guided by a teacher who both demonstrated what to do and occasionally stood back mentally from each object's familiar and functional features to consider its basic properties.

New Plan Implementation

After a reminder about the earlier whole-group session, I explained the new process. Children would watch first as I did something and then get a turn doing the very same thing on their own tray, using materials I would give to each child. I said no more before starting. I placed my tray on the table, selected a prepared twist-top bottle from a container of bottles I had stashed under my chair, and told the children they would each get a tray and a water bottle very soon, after first watching me. As I turned my bottle's top to allow water to come out, I said that I had practiced the night before, and that it was difficult at first to get only drops. "But," I said, "I practiced and learned how, and you will also learn how when you practice with your own bottle, in just a few minutes."

After placing a colored plastic chip on my tray, I twisted my bottle's top, turned it upside down, and squeezed. I intentionally twisted it too far to produce a stream of water. I said, "Oh! I twisted too much, but I can fix it, because I practiced last night." I dried the plastic chip with a sponge, commenting that "sponges soak up water very well." After adjusting my bottle's top, only a few drops emerged the next time and formed one large drop on the plastic chip. The children cheered. I asked, "What should we say about the plastic chip? Is it absorbent or not?" The children said it was not absorbent, because the large drop remained.

While using a corner of my sponge to soak up the large drop, I told the children they would soon get a sponge. I grabbed the tub of trays I'd also stored under the table and walked around to place one in front of each child. Next, I handed each child a plastic chip, with instructions to "put it on your tray." Last, I distributed the twist-top bottles, asking each child to "hold your bottle until everyone has one." Soon, children turned their bottles' twist tops and aimed for their plastic chips. Everyone practiced adjusting their bottle's twist top to release only drops. After each try, the children dried their plastic chip and surrounding tray with a sponge. After practicing, the children closed their bottles and placed them in the container I held out, after explaining they would get their bottles again after watching me demonstrate a new item. I collected their plastic chips in my outstretched hand and then started the next demonstration.

I said, "Okay, now watch," as I arranged colored wooden blocks to outline a small space on my tray and then placed a small plastic figure inside this "house." I laid a piece of lamination film on top of the house to create a "roof" that curved over it and touched the tray on both sides. The "rain" from my bottle rolled down the roof. "Wow!" the children said, giggling. When I lifted the roof to check inside, the figure was completely dry. "The lamination film repels water very well," I said. I left my house standing for children to use as a reference when building theirs.

Each child received all the needed items in a container. After transferring items to their workstations, they placed their empty container under their chair. After they built their houses and placed their figures inside, I returned the water bottles, reminding them to make a gentle rain. For the most part, they did. When asked, they also stopped the rain reasonably quickly and twisted their bottles shut. The children put their materials back in their containers, water bottles on top, and I collected them. Then, they sponged the water from their trays. Given the large amount of water this time, I traded dry pieces of sponge for those too saturated to work

After observing that two drops remained atop the aluminum foil I tested next, children declared it "not absorbent." I said, "Just like the lamination film and plastic chips." Then I used a paper towel stick to dry the drops. The sticks were quarter sheets of toweling rolled tightly and secured with masking tape near their ends. When I put one end in a drop of water, it wicked up and disappeared quickly. I placed the other end in the second drop, with the same result. Everyone agreed that the paper towel sticks were very absorbent. After the children used these materials, I collected their materials, but asked this time that they place their closed bottles beside their trays. I thought it was now unlikely that anyone would fiddle with water bottles during a demonstration.

Next, I put a piece of construction paper, a square of terry cloth, a wooden block, and a metal lid on my tray. After squeezing a water drop onto the construction paper, I asked the children what they saw. One child said, "It's not soaking in." They concluded that the construction paper was not absorbent. In contrast, they shouted, "It's absorbent!" after the water drops quickly disappeared into the terry cloth. I asked what they thought would happen to drops I planned to place on the wooden block and metal lid. "They are hard and the water can't break in," one child explained. The prediction was confirmed by observation.

Then I asked the children to look again at the construction paper, because a wet spot had formed around what remained of the water drop. "Hmmm," I said. "Should we change our mind about the construction paper?" One child said, "It is a little bit soaking it." Another added, "But not very fast." I left the construction paper on the tray to check again later and placed a paper plate on both ends of the table, each with three of the four items I had just tested. I asked the children to take just one of each kind, and they did. After testing the items, children twisted their bottle tops closed and put these and the sponges in a container I offered. They put back all tested items on their trays, except the construction paper, which they shoved to one corner for me to collect and put on the paper plate from which they had taken their supplies, for checking later. While the construction paper pieces sat on the paper plates, the children dried their trays with items from among several I had offered: wads of paper toweling, pieces of lamination film, sponges, and cotton-tipped sticks (i.e., Q-tips). No one selected lamination film. They knew it would not work. The sponges, completely familiar, could not compete with the Q-tips. But because drying an entire tray with Q-tips is a slow process, the children soon selected wads of paper toweling to help finish the job.

What made the difference? The first plan had required high levels of behavioral regulation, which is the ability to focus attention and follow directions, while inhibiting familiar and preferred behavior.[3] Most preschool-age children are still developing self-regulation, and children who have experienced continuous stress and trauma typically have lower levels than other preschool-age children.[4] Most children attending this school lived in families with very low incomes, which is a major risk factor for both stress and trauma. The revised plan provided more structure as a scaffold for helping children regulate their behavior. Using a more manageable tool to dispense water and giving the children time to practice helped them feel competent from the start. In the original implementation, the teacher provided only a very brief verbal orientation, while the revised plan included demonstrations and explanations throughout.[5] Moreover, the playful and concrete approach to the concepts captured the children's attention and maintained their interest.

Distributing materials as needed prevented concern among the children about not getting a fair share, and eliminated the negative reactions that occur when children feel slighted. The opportunity for the children to select materials from a supply for three children came near the end, when trust was high, and the materials were also organized to communicate visually that there were enough for everyone. The children also selected items, at the very end, to dry their trays. I also distributed items (e.g., workstation trays, house-building items) quickly and to the next child at the table, not by judging which child was sitting the most quietly. "Pick and choose" approaches take more time, which gives wigglers more opportunity to wiggle. Comparing and judging children also sometimes increases inappropriate behavior, because the children not yet chosen often use misbehavior to lure the teacher into giving them attention. Saying "You won't get a tray if you don't sit quietly" is ineffective; the whole point is for children to have a tray and participate. Otherwise, they lose an opportunity to learn.

Of course, a teacher's experience affects organizational skill, approaches to preventing unwanted behavior, and an activity's pace. A novice must contemplate each next step, while an experienced teacher does not deliberate at every turn. Most of all, an experienced teacher has a comfort level with children. Though each child, and each group of children, is unique, each new group of children and previous groups share similarities. I had also learned the important lesson from the finger-painting disaster that, even though children come to preschool with inappropriate behavior, a teacher has considerable control over changing it. I knew there was a good chance to succeed with the revised plan.

IMPLICATIONS FOR INSTRUCTIONAL LEADERS

For older children, textbooks are organized to provide prerequisite knowledge for what comes later; for younger children, thinking about necessary prerequisites for an activity rests with the preK teacher. Prepared plans in a curriculum guide don't indicate that the turkey baster and plastic squeeze bottles, suggested for water play several weeks before this small science activity, would help the children learn more quickly how to use the eyedropper. Sometimes the teacher does not even order small turkey basters. Instructional leaders can help teachers figure out the interconnections among materials recommended in plans. In well-managed classrooms, preK teachers also orient children to activities using demonstrations and explanations.[6] A beginning teacher might not realize how essential this is with children who have not had much previous experience of this kind.

Nothing is more challenging for an instructional leader than supporting beginning teachers, especially when children present significant challenges. Because a teacher's confidence can erode quickly, intervening early is essential. Increasing a teacher's understanding that children's behavior depends in large part on conditions within the teacher's control is also essential, though difficult. The finger-painting debacle helped me view many harder lessons that followed as challenges to meet, not as permanent and insurmountable barriers. Short of somehow demonstrating with the teacher's own children that this is true, it may be hard to change a teacher's view. Co-teaching can also work, and a principal or coach might try that.

Instructional leaders are not being helpful by insisting that a struggling new teacher implement prepared materials and plans with fidelity.

The teacher in this example got into difficulty because she trusted a plan written by an "expert" (Judy). The plan included no warning that it might not work, no advice about judging the likelihood that it would, and no information about how to increase the odds of succeeding. Both beginners and experienced teachers, no matter what age children they teach, need good professional development (PD) that helps them judge how to modify plans.[7] Good PD includes in-classroom support. Administrators might find consultants and coaches who can teach by example and analyze with teachers what worked and didn't. After experience with administrators who assigned specific classroom tasks for my visits (e.g., read a story and manage a follow-up activity; conduct a small-group session), I found it difficult to ever again provide PD to a group without also spending time in the classroom.

PART II

Preschoolers Learn Through Play

Until about thirty years ago, Center Time in preK was called "free play." As the name implies, children could choose where and how to spend much of their time while at preschool. When free play prevailed, learning to read and do basic math were saved for first grade, with both kindergarten and preK expected to support motor and social development through routines of daily living and child-initiated play. PreK educators did not worry then about supporting children's readiness for academic learning because they assumed that children's intellectual capacities would unfold in concert with each child's individual, genetically determined timetable for neural-ripening.

Many of the assumptions that play proponents made in that era are inconsistent with today's science. For example, research has disputed the claim that the young child cannot see or hear well enough to meet the demands of learning to read.[1] Of course, broad experiences contribute to overall oral language and content knowledge, and support interest and engagement, but research has established that the capacity to see and hear very small differences exists early in infancy. The preschool child's lack of response to small differences among letters is a concept development issue (i.e., knowing that small differences matter), not a physical and perceptual growth issue.[2] Similarly, conscious awareness of individual sounds in words (i.e., phonological awareness) is not simply a matter of hearing, but requires learning that spoken words comprise individual sounds and paying attention to these when spelling words and reading them.[3]

When the view that genetics and maturation mostly controlled development gradually gave way to the view that experience is central to both general intellectual development and specific academic learning, commitments were made to closing the achievement gap between lower-income children and their more economically secure peers. By the late 1990s, when early learning standards became available, kindergarten teachers began to devote more effort to academic skills, and play and other child-directed activities began to decline.[4] PreK classrooms also began to include library corners, listening posts, writing centers, and areas with literacy and math materials. Whole-group story time and group circle time were also added to the daily schedule in preK, and a small-groups time was used in some programs to support oral vocabulary, and literacy and math skill development.

In half-day preK programs, small groups were often held concurrently with Center Time, which required children to stop playing when called to their ten- to fifteen-minute session. Children's play was disrupted not only when they were called for a turn in small groups, but also when classmates were called for theirs and then returned. Moreover, teachers, busy now with planning for teacher-directed, academic learning segments of the preK day, no longer devoted as much time as they once had to planning for child-directed play. Supporting children, as they played, also declined in programs where one teacher's time was consumed entirely by small-group instruction at Center Time.

Developmentally appropriate practice (DAP) documents continued to emphasize the importance of the whole child and a balance between child-directed and teacher-directed experiences.[5] The American Academy of Pediatrics also published an extensive review of research about the many benefits of play.[6] Yet, despite these efforts, the trend toward less time for play and more for teacher-directed, academic instruction continues apace in many preK classrooms. The tide might yet turn in response to research that continues to show a strong correlation between several social skills and emotions, and academic achievement (e.g., self-regulation/effortful control, executive functioning, feelings of hope joy, pride).[7]

These findings, coupled with the report of long-term negative outcomes (i.e., through the end of third grade) in the statewide, Voluntary Prekindergarten Program in Tennessee (TN-VPK), have increased concern about the balance between teacher-directed and child-directed activity in preK.[8] The TN-VPK data showed that the intervention children's preK day was dominated by whole-group, teacher-directed activities, with only half as much time spent in child-directed centers, including play, and that children had almost no time for active motor play on a playground or in a gym. The study's authors suggested that the shift to more teacher-directed, academic instruction in preK left too little time for child-directed play and hands-on activities, experiences likely to benefit the social skills that predict academic achievement.[9]

We share this heightened concern, which compelled us to devote several chapters in this book to play. Chapter 6 focuses on socio-dramatic play and adult roles in supporting it, and includes a general review of the benefits of child-directed socio-dramatic play. Chapter 7 describes a small-group, teacher-guided and teacher-directed play store that supports number understandings, social skills, and oral language—an example of how play can be combined with skill building. Chapter 8 illustrates how preK teachers and principals might work through questions concerning the place of play in learning.

CHAPTER 6

They fall off trees, I guess.

Socio-dramatic Play

RAYMOND TAPPED A PLASTIC EGG on the side of the frying pan, then pulled it open and dumped it into the pan. After cracking and dumping two more eggs, Raymond stirred in the pan with a wooden spoon, stopping occasionally to turn a knob on the stove, as if adjusting the burner. The teacher helping children at the art and water tables glanced over occasionally to observe Raymond in the playhouse. When she found time, she paid a visit.

Teacher. What are you cooking? (*Sits down at the small table.*)

Raymond. Some eggs.

Teacher. Oh, eggs. Making breakfast?

Raymond. Uh-huh.

Teacher. Where do eggs come from?

Raymond. The refrigerator.

Teacher. Well, before that?

Raymond. From the store. You buy 'em there. Nana does.

Teacher. Oh, I see. But where does the store get them?

Raymond turned around this time to share his thinking: "They fall off trees, I guess." With that, he grabbed the frying pan by its handle, walked to the table to set it down near the teacher, and said, "You can eat these." Then, he left the playhouse.

The teacher's first two questions were at least consistent with Raymond's play theme of cooking breakfast. Her other questions not only departed from Raymond's play theme, but also moved out of a play mode into quizzing about the origin of eggs. An adult's participation can enrich children's pretend play. It's all in knowing how.

THE ADULT'S ROLE IN CHILDREN'S PRETEND PLAY

Researchers have identified four adult play styles: (1) co-player, (2) play leader, (3) stage manager, and (4) play director. The first three styles support children's pretend play, each in a different way, while the fourth undermines it.[1] A co-player and a play leader both join the play. A co-player takes care to suggest only plot ideas that fit within the child's current play frame. A play leader, in contrast, assumes a major role and offers plot ideas that sometimes take play in a new direction, though never away from the child's current theme. The stage manager and play director exert their influence from outside the play. The stage manager provides materials needed for children to enact scenarios they have planned and offers advice about how to make play plans work. In sharp contrast, a play director asks many literal questions and assigns play-related tasks, both of which control the play and interfere with children's ability to adopt roles and develop scenarios. The style of the teacher who entered Raymond's play was typical of a play director.

We illustrate the three supportive play styles using Raymond's pretend play as a starting point. Although pretend play in the preK classroom typically involves three or four children, the examples include no more than two because we designed them primarily to illustrate differences among adult play styles.

Co-Player Scenario

Teacher. Knock-knock! (*At edge of playhouse, moving hand as if knocking on a door.*)

Raymond, *looking.*

Teacher. Hi, I'm your new neighbor, Ms. Reynolds, from across the street. May I come in?

Raymond. Uh-huh.

Teacher. Looks like you are cooking. Smells good.

Raymond. I'm making breakfast.

Teacher. Sounds yummy. (*Sits down at small table.*)

Raymond, *approaching to set frying pan on table.* I'll get plates. (*Returns to cooking area; gets plates; returns to table.*) Here's yours. (*Hands plate to teacher; places second on table; sits down.*)

Teacher. Thank-you. Were you expecting someone for breakfast? I won't eat too many eggs. I had cold cereal at home before I came over.

Raymond. Nobody's coming, and I can make more.

Teacher. Okay. Thanks. (*Serves self, using wooden spoon in pan.*)

Raymond. Oh! We need forks! (*Gets forks. Hands one to teacher; keeps other. Serves self. He and teacher eat eggs.*)

Teacher. These eggs are delicious. They taste fresh from the farm. Did you get them at the farm stand right outside town?

Raymond. No. Got 'em from the refrigerator.

Teacher. Oh, I see. Somebody shopped earlier, I guess.

Elyssa, *enters; sits down.* I'm hungry too.

Raymond. I cooked eggs. Want some?

Elyssa. I'll get a plate.

Raymond. No, I'm the cooker. I'll get stuff.

Teacher, *speaking to Elyssa while Raymond gets items.* Hello, I'm Mrs. Reynolds from across the street. Are you a neighbor too?

Elyssa. No! This is my preschool! (*Laughs*) And you're a teacher!

Teacher, *whispering*. Oh, I know, but we are pretending, aren't we?

Raymond, *placing plate and fork on table near Elyssa*.

Elyssa. Well, I'm the mommy in this house.

Raymond. I'm the dad.

Teacher. And I'm the neighbor. I must leave now to go shopping. Thanks so much for the scrambled eggs.

Play Leader Scenario

Elyssa. Well, I'm the mommy in this house.

Teacher. Oh, I noticed a baby in the high chair.

Elyssa. I need a bottle. (*Gets up to search.*)

Raymond, *eats more eggs. Watches Elyssa search doll bed for doll bottle. Spoons eggs onto her plate at the table.*

Elyssa, *returns with baby, bottle in hand*. Hold these.

Teacher. Sure, I'd love to hold your baby.

Elyssa, *moves high chair to table. Takes baby doll from teacher. Puts in high chair.*

Teacher. Why don't you feed him solid food first, and then the bottle? Raymond just put scrambled eggs on your plate, and they are nice and soft for a baby.

Elyssa. Yes, I'll do eggs first. My baby likes eggs. (*Uses fork to feed baby.*)

Teacher. Hi, baby. I think you do like those eggs.

Stage Manager Scenario

Raymond, *alone, cooking eggs.*

Teacher. What are you cooking, Raymond? (*Standing outside playhouse.*)

Raymond. Eggs. I'm making breakfast. Gotta get my kid up too.

Teacher. Oh, I see.

Raymond. Yeah . . . already late for day care.

Teacher. Okay, I'll pull the high chair to the table for your baby. (*Pulls high chair over; puts baby in. Returns to water table. Keeps eye on play.*)

Raymond, *carries egg pan to table. Gets plates for self and baby, then forks. Serves eggs to self; puts eggs on baby's plate. Pretends to eat.*

Teacher. I'll see if I can find a bib. I know we have some. If he's going to day care, he can't have a dirty shirt. (*Finds bib; puts on baby.*) There! Babies are kind of messy eaters. Hope you aren't late to day care. (*Returns to water table/art table area. Keeps eye on playhouse.*)

Raymond, *eating eggs and feeding baby.* Hurry up and eat. I'm late for work.

Teacher, *searching in box of purses and bags; selects a bag. Puts bottle from doll bed in bag; adds clothing from small chest. Approaches table.*

I put a bottle and a change of clothing in the day-care bag. I know you are running late. Do you have a long drive? (*Puts bag in empty chair seat.*)

Raymond. We're very late. We are laaaate!

Teacher, *returning to water table and art area; keeps eye on playhouse.*

The teacher's attentiveness to the children's play themes kept the play going. Adults also support children's play with materials and by preparing children for new play themes. We discuss these topics next.

MATERIAL SUPPORT FOR DRAMATIC PLAY

A playhouse with basic supplies supported Raymond and Elyssa's enactment of familiar roles. Teachers can enrich home and family play by adding new items and can create settings for other themes, such as a doctor's office, restaurant, post office, or aquarium. For each new theme, teachers help children prepare for new roles.

Extending Home and Family Play

The playhouse had a sink, stove, and refrigerator. It also had a shelving unit with dishes, cooking pans, mixing bowls, and cooking utensils. The refrigerator was stocked with food, and additional food cartons sat on top of the shelving unit. The playhouse also had a doll bed and a baby doll, a chest of drawers with doll clothes, and dress-up clothes for the children. Though well stocked with basic materials, a teacher could add new items over time to extend the play. For example, small, empty squeeze-type bottles of dish detergent and a dish towel would encourage additional play at the sink. A recipe book, with pictures and a few words, might prompt new food-preparation scenarios. A pad of paper and a pencil often encourage children to scribble shopping lists, and additional feeding items and playthings for the babies could extend children's baby-care options.

As the teacher adds props gradually to a play setting, she can introduce them in the daily Introduction to Centers. A teacher might introduce new burping cloths for the playhouse like this:

> There are dolls in the house play area, as always, and baby bottles. [*Teacher has doll and bottle in hand.*] But, today, you'll also find new burping cloths. I'll put one on my shoulder and then hold my baby up and pat his back, which helps get air out of his tummy. Air coming up is called burping. When babies burp, they sometimes spit up a bit of milk, and that can stain our clothes. If you want to protect your clothes from spit-up, you can use a burping cloth when feeding your baby.

A few days later, a teacher might introduce a sectioned baby dish and several empty, plastic baby-food jars labeled pears, beets, green beans, and so on. The teacher again explains and role-plays the items' uses in Introduction to Centers:

> As babies get older, they eat very soft food, because babies don't have teeth to chew food like we do. Here's a baby dish, divided into sections (*points to*), and you could put pears in one section (*shows jar; underlines label*), and maybe green beans in a different section, and then use a spoon to feed your baby. Babies need padded spoons, like this one (*holds up*). And don't forget a bib to keep your baby's clothes clean. It goes around a baby's neck. This bib has an easy fastener on the back. Just press it together (*turns doll around; fastens bib*).

When introducing board books for the babies, a teacher might suggest visiting the classroom library:

> I put small board books in this basket for our library, and this sign on it says, "BABY BOOKS." You can pretend that the library is just down the street from the playhouse. Remember the librarian who visited a few weeks ago and talked to your parents in a night meeting? Some of you now have library cards. Well, our playhouse library cards say, "The Corner Preschool Children," and anyone can use one. You'll find them on top of the refrigerator.

Supporting More Play Themes

Preparing for other play themes can follow a similar process. For a doctor's office, many items are necessary at the start (e.g., stethoscope, otoscope, syringe for shots, patient charts, appointment cards), while others can be added later (e.g., eye-checking chart, reflex hammer, blood pressure cuff). Before setting up a new play area, teachers can read relevant books at read-aloud time to acquaint children with roles, associated behavior, and key vocabulary (e.g., stethoscope, otoscope, syringe, vaccination, prescription, pharmacy). In addition to reading books, a field trip is also useful for some play settings (e.g., post office, aquarium).

As children first play in a new setting, a teacher typically does some stage managing and joins the play as well. For example, when co-playing as a patient, the teacher helps children understand and perform their roles (e.g., "My ear has been hurting. Can you look at it? I see that you have an otoscope over there.") Most play settings are available for three or four weeks, which helps to ensure that children have opportunities to play a variety of roles in the setting, and teachers can make turns lists to support role rotation among the children. Typically, a teacher returns to the playhouse with its home and family theme, in between other settings, and these are good times to add a few new items.

Choosing Pretend Play Locations

Sometimes, the playhouse area can be transformed into a new play setting. At other times, it is maintained. For example, without a house area, children have nowhere to go after taking a baby to the doctor, and no place to dress up before going out to dinner. The block area is often used for a new play setting, while the house play area stays intact. In one classroom, the house play area was included in aquarium play at the block area by taking babies on a trip to the aquarium. The children continued to feed babies and dress babies, put them to bed for a nap, and so on, but the pretend aquarium allowed something new for their home and family play.

A tabletop provides another option for pretend play and requires much less space than settings where the children enact roles themselves. In the tabletop context, child players use small figures, small blocks, and other materials to build rooms of houses and even outdoor play equipment for a backyard. Commercially made blocks designed as storefronts or other buildings (e.g., hospital, library, post office, fire station) can also be used. Children drive small cars, or move a fire truck, ambulance, or mail truck, while imagining the community helper inside. Small community helper figures (e.g., mail carrier, sanitation worker, firefighter) could also be added, along with props, such as garbage cans (i.e., cylinder blocks from a small unit block set) and a fire hose (piece of small-diameter plastic tubing).

Because tables are often used for something else during other times of the day, children typically assemble the setting each day and then put items away at cleanup time. Setting up adds an interesting cognitive challenge, which children typically enjoy. In tabletop settings, a child can use more than one figure. This involves a cognitive stance that differs from the stance a child takes when enacting one role in a typical pretend play setting. Each child playing at the tabletop can also coordinate the multiple roles of the figures with roles of figures enacted by another child. This cognitive activity is challenging, yet children are motivated to engage in it.

HOW PRETEND PLAY BENEFITS CHILDREN

Studies of pretend play have found some benefits related to the quality and quantity of adult interactions in the play. For example, children talk more in pretend play when adult utterances mostly continue in the direction of the child's play, rather than change it.[2] Language outcomes are also related to the quantity of child-child talk. Dramatic play often prompts considerable child-child talk, because, with three or four children playing, they must discuss roles and scenarios and then talk when enacting their roles.[3] In the aggregate, research suggests that pretend play benefits children's oral vocabulary development, comprehension and production of narratives, and use of literacy routines (e.g., making shopping lists, reading books to babies, consulting a cookbook, looking at grocery store ads).[4]

Other benefits to children's learning are mediated by the social skills that children use and develop as they engage in pretend play. For example, researchers have found significant relationships between preschoolers' positive engagement in pretend play and their engagement in teacher-guided and teacher-directed learning activities. In contrast, children who are passive bystanders in play are often less engaged in learning activities with a teacher, while disruptive players often have lower attention in learning situations and less persistence in learning tasks.[5] These results suggest that helping preschool-age children who are disconnected from, or disruptive in, play to engage more positively in play might improve relationships with both peers and teachers, which, in turn, might improve academic performance.

An intervention study designed to improve the peer play of pre-school-age children with a history of abuse and neglect used trained parent volunteers and a positive classmate as a partner in a small dramatic play center set up for use during the daily Center Time. This intervention produced a significant change in target children's social behavior. Although the researchers did not study the effects on the children's academic learning, they did note that many studies have identified the absence of social play skills as a risk factor for academic success.[6] Even though correlational studies do not allow us to conclude that improving social skills through play will improve a child's academic performance, it might be worth a try.

IMPLICATIONS FOR INSTRUCTIONAL LEADERS

Because pretend play does not address assessment accountability items as directly as instructional contexts that focus solely on academic skills, many instructional leaders have pushed for more whole-group, teacher-directed instruction and less child-selected activity. But this new allocation of time in preK may be shortsighted. One explanation for why academic gains made in preK often fade over time, while control children might catch up and even surpass the intervention group, is that programs dominated by teacher-directed academic instruction, especially when it is narrowly focused in literacy or math skills, might not engage children or develop their interest in learning to the same extent as more balanced programming. Programs dominated by teacher-directed, whole-group instruction also might not support self-regulation and persistence to the same extent as more balanced programming.[7] Instructional leaders should try to establish a reasonable balance in preK classrooms between whole-group, teacher-directed instruction and activities that are child initiated and teacher supported, including play.

It is also wise to keep in mind that before literacy and math skills became a major priority in preK, over the past two decades preK teachers learned how to support children's play in preservice preparation programs. Today, teachers who seek early childhood licensure for preK through second or third grade have little if any preparation in this area. This situation suggests that some preK teachers might be vulnerable to filling the day with academic learning. For this reason, professional development offerings for preK teachers should include dramatic play. The inclusion of information and discussion about how play can support the development of oral language, content knowledge, and social skills helps teachers understand that devoting some time to play is likely to aid overall learning, not diminish it.

CHAPTER 7

I want a dog, a marble, and a little horse.

Small-Group Guided Play

JACOB SAID, "I WANT A DOG, a marble, and a little horse," as he started his first turn in the tabletop store with five pennies in front of him. "Let's think about this," his teacher suggested. "You want a dog (*points to price on a sign*). How much does one cost?" Jacob looked, but said nothing. "Two pennies," the teacher read while underlining both numeral and word on the sign that read "2 PENNIES." After helping Jacob push two pennies away from his group of five, she asked, "How much does each marble cost?" Jacob looked as the teacher pointed to its sign, "1 PENNY," and answered, "One." He pushed one penny from the three remaining from his original five toward the two already committed to the dog. When the teacher asked how many pennies were left and gestured toward them, Jacob quickly said, "Two." The teacher confirmed that the horse cost six pennies (*points to price*) and then said, "So, two . . . three, four, five, six . . . Six is a lot more than two." She wiggled the four fingers she had raised to tally the distance between two and six, while counting, and explained: "You can buy a horse on your next turn, when you get five more pennies." Amanda commented that Jacob could buy another dog. The teacher agreed, but asked whether Jacob would have enough pennies to buy a horse on his next turn. Amanda said he wouldn't, but would if he bought another marble or a Popsicle stick for only one penny.

The teacher asked Jacob whether he wanted to spend one penny now and save one to help buy the horse next time, or save both. "I'll keep these," Jacob said. "Okay, now please give me two pennies for the dog." Jacob picked them up. "Thank-you," said the salesclerk. Jacob picked up the remaining penny from the committed pile, explaining, "for my marble." After thanking Jacob again and giving him the marble, the teacher announced that Amanda would play customer next, and Terrance would get his turn after that.

Amanda purchased a small car and a little cat, at two pennies each. She had eyed a coin purse ("4 PENNIES") for a moment, pulling one penny away from the original group of five, while thinking. Realizing she could not buy a car or a cat with only one penny remaining if she bought a purse, she chose two items now and saved one penny, explaining, "I can buy a purse next time and something else too. Or, maybe two if they are just one penny." Terrance spent his five pennies on ·a little helicopter and a small bear, for two and three pennies, respectively. He recognized the numerals on the price signs and quickly shoved pennies for each item to the committed-to-purchase pile. After moving the three pennies for the bear toward the two pennies committed to the helicopter, Terrance seemed disappointed and said, "Oh, I wanted a marble, too, like Jacob." The teacher explained that he could either buy one on his next turn or rethink this turn's purchases. Terrance stuck with his original decision, saying, "I really like those bears." With the first round of turns over, the teacher distributed five more pennies to each child, inviting everyone to count along as she placed them, one at a time, on the table in front of each child.

PLAY STORE SETUP AND PROCEDURES

At the play store, items were displayed on trays; their prices, which ranged from one penny to seven, sat beside them on tent-style signs. At the start of each day's play, the teacher named each kind of item and read a few prices before dispensing pennies. On some days, the teacher added a few new items and removed others, always providing enough to make the store interesting. Three children played at one time, in a twenty-five-minute session; two groups could play during Center Time. The play store was available for about two weeks, periodically throughout the year, and children could always add their names to the list of those who wanted a turn.

Typically, the three children in a group differed in number-related knowledge and skill, which made a session move along faster than if all, or even two, had only very rudimentary skills. After a few months, a teacher sometimes chose three children, all with well-developed number skills for the same group; eliminated items costing only one or two pennies; added items priced at eight, nine, or ten pennies; and kept penny allotment per turn at five. These changes increased the children's thinking about numbers, especially when planning expensive purchases.

For the first few months of school, a second teacher had to manage the remaining children in other centers, because the teacher playing in the store was too busy to help. If children received speech and language services in the classroom, the specialist was scheduled for Center Time on store days. Volunteers also sometimes helped, and in one full-day program, teachers opened only a few centers during afternoon Center Time to make supervision more manageable for one teacher. Usually, by midyear, a few children were skilled enough to serve as salesclerk for two or three classmates. A teacher kept an eye on the activity, helping as needed, but also had time to assist in nearby centers. By the last few months of a year, store materials for two children could be placed on a tray at the puzzles and manipulatives table for independent use during Center Time. Two shoppers recruited a third child to serve as salesclerk, or someone wanting to play salesclerk recruited two shoppers.

WHAT CHILDREN LEARNED BY PLAYING STORE

Store play supports the development of number understanding, social skills, and oral language. Number-related skills include reciting number words in order, counting a group of items to determine its quantity, and understanding that the last number word said when counting a set indicates its quantity (i.e., the cardinality concept). Children also develop a general idea of the effect after taking items from, or adding items to, a set and acquire some knowledge of number relationships (e.g., four is one more than three, and one less than five). Learning to read numerals up to ten and associate these with their quantities rounds out early number knowledge and helps bridge informal mathematics to symbol-based, formal mathematics.[1]

As the descriptions of store play illustrate, many number skills are integrated as children purchase items. Children are also highly motivated to attend to a teacher's instruction and feedback. The pricing scheme, in combination with a five-penny-per-turn allotment, motivates children to combine pennies from more than one turn to purchase higher-priced items. In other words, children engage in a variety of number-related procedures as they play store, and these prompt thinking about number and help them develop some basic number-related skills, such as counting. Children also learn to take turns, delay gratification, and persist. They also change tasks several times. For example, they move pennies from the initial group to a group of pennies committed to purchases and from the committed group to the salesclerk's hand, and at the end of a turn, they switch from playing actively as a customer to watching and thinking about a classmate's play. These changes likely increase children's ability to regulate their behavior, which is a predictor of later school achievement.[2]

Oral language development is also supported in this small-group context, such as when children name items to buy, announce and explain changes in their decisions, and share thoughts about peers' purchases.[3] As the teacher gives directions and provides explanations, children hear mature grammar and new words, some that are number-related (e.g., numeral, more, count, one more, one less, add to, combine, first, second, next, last), others that are store-related (e.g., customer, price, cost, expensive, purchase, buy, pay for, clerk), and others that are terms for politeness (thank-you, please). Multiple use of new terms in a meaningful context is an ideal condition for vocabulary learning. The small-group play activity also involves some complexity because several different number understandings are used together when a child takes a turn. Children who are waiting for a turn also observe and become cognitively engaged in the decisions and possibilities of the child taking a turn.[4] Thus, all children in the small group are learning during the entire session, not only when taking their turn.

MONITORING PROGRESS IN NUMBER SKILL ACQUISITION

A small guided- or directed-play setting allows the teacher-salesclerk to observe what children know about number and use this information to support further learning. We consider here the behavior of two children in the play store example to illustrate observational data collection and its use in planning experiences for each child.

Jacob's Number Skills

Jacob did not respond when the teacher pointed to "2" on the price sign for the dog, but did say "one" when she pointed to the marble's price. We don't know whether he could read "3," "4," or "5," because he was not interested in items at those prices. We also don't know whether he could read "6," because the teacher read the horse's price without asking Jacob first. Jacob did understand quantities stipulated by the number words "one" and "two," because he moved two pennies for the dog and one for the marble, and, when asked, said "two" pennies remained from his five-penny allotment. Jacob also gave the teacher two pennies when she requested payment for the dog and picked them up from the three pennies remaining in that group, by just eyeing rather than counting items (i.e., determined quantity by subitizing).[5]

On his next turn, not described in the example, Jacob bought the horse first after the teacher pointed to the horses and their price, saying, "Horses cost six pennies." Jacob pushed pennies away from his initial stash of seven (i.e., two saved plus five from this turns allotment), as he counted, but recited number words up through four after having moved only three. The teacher said she'd double-check and quickly recounted the first three pennies, touching each one. Then, she said, "Four . . . ," and voiced it longer than usual, while looking at Jacob to signal that he should move another penny. She continued to support his counting as he moved the fifth and sixth pennies. Because each next number word in the counting sequence is linked very tightly to the previous one, a novice counter's recall often falters if number words are recited slowly. By counting along, an adult provides the necessary support.

Based on Jacob's behavior, his teacher probably continued to group him with children who had greater skill, knowing he still needed considerable teacher help and more time to take his turn than children with more skill. By grouping children in this way, the teacher could make sure each group's turn stayed within the twenty-five-minutes planned, which allowed a second group also to have a turn during Center Time on the same day. The teacher also probably used other opportunities during the day to give Jacob more exposure to the number word sequence. Although number word recitation (i.e., rote counting) can be overdone and does not by itself lead to meaningful counting, learning the number word sequence requires exposure and practice. The teacher might go to the block area during cleanup when Jacob is there and hand blocks of a kind to put away, counting as she transfers blocks to Jacob's hand. Jacob's teacher might also send a few books home with Jacob for family members to read with him.[6]

Amanda's Number Skills

Amanda demonstrated considerable skill. For example, she moved one penny away from the four she considered for a purse, without overtly counting the four. When deciding to purchase only a car and a cat at two pennies each and save one penny for next time, Amanda realized she'd have enough pennies for both a purse and another item, "if it is two pennies," or for two items, if only one penny each, "like a marble."

This comment revealed good knowledge of part-whole relationships for small numbers, which she also demonstrated in her comments to the teacher about Jacob's purchasing options. The teacher could get a copy of *12 Ways to Get to 11* from the school or local public library to send home with Amanda.[7] Her teacher might also make sure that some of the number-related items at the puzzles and literacy and math skills centers are suitable for Amanda.

OTHER NUMBER EXPERIENCES

Preschoolers need experiences in addition to store play in order to develop number skills, given each child's relatively short time playing store and this context's restricted range of numerals to read and sets to count. Some additional experiences arise spontaneously in the classroom. The challenge is to exploit them for a child's benefit. For example, suppose a child announces one day at the snack or lunch table that his brother just had a birthday and is now six. Instead of saying, "Oh, really, wow. He's getting old, isn't he?" a teacher might ask how many years older his brother is. The child might know that six is two more than four, but if not, the teacher can prompt the child to raise four fingers for his age and, from there, count up to six while the teacher raises a finger to tally the two increments beyond four. "He's two more older than me," the child might report, as the teacher wiggles her two fingers. Another child at the table might continue the sibling birthday topic by reporting that she is four years older than a baby brother. But the teacher, who knows the baby is already two, might help the child calculate the difference: "Your baby brother is two. Let's figure out how much older you are." The teacher holds up two fingers for the baby brother's age and then counts to four, raising two more fingers. She wiggles these as she asks, "So, how many years older are you?" The child sees that she is two, not four, years older.

Other number situations arise routinely in a preK classroom. For example, when one child has the container of vehicles in the block area and another wants some, they must divide the items. This can be done by eye, with follow-up counting and comparing of the items in the two sets. Or the child with the container could alternate giving one item to the other child and himself, until the basket is empty. Signs indicating the number of children in areas also provide more daily number experiences. Children can consult these signs when they want to enter a center.

Several number-related items should also be available at the puzzles or manipulatives center. These can include puzzles with numerals and pictures in groups to match; boards with one to ten in their left-hand column and an open space to the right to place the quantity of cubes or buttons that matches; a staircase frame with a row of ten columns that allows a child to place one cube in the first, two in the second, and so on, to ten. Each column has a label at the top with the appropriate numeral. With prompting, children notice that two is one more than one, three is one more than two, and so on. Even a one-hundreds grid, with a one-hundreds numeral grid lining is worth having at this center. Although most early-learning state standards stipulate that children should learn to count accurately to ten by the end of preK and also on their way toward counting to twenty, exposure can be broader. Preschoolers at first enjoy just filling the one-hundreds tray with cubes and learn quite a lot when a teacher says, "I wonder how many cubes you just put in that top row? Shall we count and see?" After counting, the teacher might lift the last cube or ask the child to and read the numeral. Over time, a teacher can comment that the last numeral printed in the second row is twenty, that this many cubes are in two full rows, and do the same with thirty and beyond, as appropriate.

Sometimes, something unexpected happens with a one-hundreds grid. For example, a child who was approaching his fifth birthday was filling the second row in the grid, after having filled the first. After noticing more 5's below in the column where he was about to place a cube over 15, he pointed to each one, saying, "There's my 5!" A teacher who approached realized what he was talking about, explained that "his" 5 was in the first row and lifted the cube to reveal it. She explained that 5 in the next row was part of 15 and suggested they count to make sure there were ten cubes in the top row. After doing that, the teacher said, "Okay, now let's count here." She and the child counted cubes on top of 11, 12, 13, and 14. The teacher summarized, saying, "So, there are ten in the top row, and when you get to 15 here in the second, that's five more cubes than ten. When the second row is full, there are twenty cubes in the tray, and when you keep filling rows, there are more and more." She read twenty-five, thirty-five, forty-five, and so on, all the way down to ninety-five. "So, only the 5 up in the first row matches your next birthday."

Although this child probably comprehended only part of what the teacher explained, the instructional guidance might prompt him to notice six in numerals in the next column, seven in numerals in the next, and so on. And when a preschooler can count to twenty, thirty, forty, as sometimes happens, the child can see what these numbers look like on the one-hundreds tray. Researchers who have considered the effects of explanations suggest that even though not completely understood, they "provide constraints for a child's theory building," and that small changes in thinking in multiple contexts over time are involved in learning anything that involves complexity.[8]

IMPLICATIONS FOR INSTRUCTIONAL LEADERS

It is not possible or necessary to engage children in situations every day with the level of instructional richness the play store offers. If repeatedly offered a few times a week for a couple of weeks at a time throughout the year, the experience can optimize children's number learning because it brings different skills together in a way that supports a child in connecting them. In a small-group setting, a teacher can help according to each child's needs by modeling and providing verbal explanations.

The biggest challenge in using a small-group play setting during Center Time is the staffing. With just two teachers and many centers open, it is difficult. Instructional leaders can discuss possible solutions with preK teachers and perhaps arrange for volunteers to help or discuss with specialists the possibility of delivering some services in the classroom at these times, as we noted earlier. Sometimes, older children in the building visit kindergarten classes to read to children. If their schedules allow, older children might read to some preschoolers in the book area during Center Time, which would help reduce the supervision load on the second teacher.

CHAPTER 8

Eliza has her own way of doing things.

Playing with Learning

THE PRINCIPAL WAS ON HER MORNING WALK through the building's eight classrooms just as four-year-old Eliza began to sign in on her classroom's "Look Who's Here Today" chart. Eliza happily provided a running account of her actions when the principal stopped to watch. After writing *E*, she announced, "That's my letter, Eliza!" After *L*, she said, "That's Lisa, my mommy." She left some space after *L* and then wrote *A*, exclaiming, "*A*! That's Ali's letter. She's my best friend!" Then, she returned to the empty space between *L* and *A*, to add *I* "with a dot," and then *Z*, her flat, wavy squiggle.

When finished, Eliza walked quickly to the dramatic play area where Ali was waiting, but the principal lingered before picking up the chart and approaching the teacher. "I'm wondering why . . . ," she began, but the teacher jumped in to finish her sentence: "She skipped to the end and then went back to fill in, right? She has her own way of doing things and always has reasons. That's Eliza!" Knowing that this was not a good time to talk, the principal asked to discuss this situation later in the morning, after the children had gone home. The teacher said that she could.

THE PRINCIPAL'S THINKING

Although the principal saw Eliza form all the letters in her name and put each where it belonged, it troubled her that Eliza wrote the letters out of order. She also wondered why the teacher hadn't encouraged Eliza to write "E-L-I-Z-A" straightforwardly, given her awareness of Eliza's unusual approach. The principal thought children should get feedback when they did something incorrectly. The principal's other concern was that she hadn't seen the puzzles this morning that all preK teachers in the building had designed in the summer professional development session and agreed to use. Had this teacher never used them, or had she tried without success? The principal thought the name puzzles could provide exactly the instruction that Eliza needed. A teacher named each letter, in order, when putting a child's puzzle pieces out on the table, then repeated the names with the child, as the puzzle was assembled. This strategy helped children learn the names of letters in their names and then to recall them later, in the correct order, when writing their names.

THE TEACHER'S THINKING

Eliza's teacher was accustomed to the principal's brief morning visits, to finding the sticky note comments she left on her desk, and to occasional requests to meet later in the morning during the time always set aside for teachers. But the principal's immediate question today conveyed an unusual sense of urgency. The teacher was surprised that the principal was concerned about Eliza's approach to writing her name, because she already knew about Eliza's tendency to put her own spin on things. For example, the teaching team had told the principal about the time Eliza tested all the paint colors on her hands, for several weeks, before painting on the easel paper. Eliza's name-writing approach was consistent with her personality and history. Besides, by the end, each letter was in its correct place to spell *ELIZA*.

THE MEETING

After cordial greetings, the principal began to describe what she had noticed and what concerned her about Eliza's name-writing:

> Eliza seemed happy to sign in and concentrated on the task. She also acknowledged my presence and commented about each letter she wrote. She certainly formed these letters quite legibly, and although she named only *A*, she probably knows the other letters' names. My concern is that Eliza wrote *A* before backing up to write *I* and *Z*. I worry that doing this every day might lead to writing *ELA*, and then just adding *Z* and *I*, or *I* and *Z*, at the end (*ELAIZ*). Or, if she doesn't leave enough space, she might put only *Z* in the space and *I* at the end (*ELAZI*). Do you think there's a potential for these problems?

The teacher said no, but admitted that, in all honesty, she hadn't thought about it. In her view, Eliza liked to explore, experiment, and play with almost everything and was curious, capable, and socially savvy. Although the teacher thought the principal probably remembered Eliza's characteristics from previous discussions with the teaching team, she decided a review might help:

> In Preschool 1, Eliza often insisted on her own way of doing something, rather than following a teacher's request. But because Eliza's noncompliance was usually followed by acceptance within a few minutes, in rare instances, within a few days, we agreed not to squish her desire to make sense of things or stifle her unique approach to new tasks. We saw Eliza's behavior as mostly a strength and agreed to insist on compliance, straightaway, only when necessary. I see her name-writing approach in the same light. So far, the letters end up in the correct sequence. Can you say more about your concern?

The principal repeated that Eliza's process could become a habit. Specifically, she might come to associate *A* as following *L*, not *Z*, and then write her name *ELAIZ* or just *ELA*. The principal thought it made more sense to insist that Eliza write the letters in order as they appear in her name and didn't think experimenting was appropriate in situations where only one way is correct. She ended by asking, "Isn't name-writing something to just do in a certain way?"

Hoping to allay the principal's concern, the teacher reviewed Eliza's approach to writing her name when first learning how:

> Eliza's mother told us that after writing *L*, Eliza often hesitated and asked, "Is it the line, Mommy?" (*referring to the I*). And before writing *Z*, she often asked, "How do I make that squiggly-wiggly one?" After several weeks of concentrating and asking questions about letter order and formation, Eliza knew the letters' order and could form them legibly enough for others to read. Her current experimentation started several weeks later, after she had become familiar with names of friends and family members. She soon noticed that first letters in some of their names were used someplace in hers, and that's when she started commenting about those letters and writing them first, leaving space to write other letters later. Her new approach didn't surprise me, because close relationships are important to Eliza, and she always experiments and plays with whatever she is learning. She is also very observant and quick in making connections.

The conversation went back and forth a while longer, but the principal's worries remained. In the interest of time, the principal raised her other concern, the name puzzles, asking, "Have you used them?" She also expressed her view that chanting the letters in their correct order, twice, would reinforce letter names and their correct order when Eliza wrote it. She also noticed that Eliza had named only *A* that morning and asked if she could name the other four. She said, "Maybe you could explain to me how the name puzzles fit into your teaching of letter names."

The teacher reported that for the first two months of school, children did the puzzles every day, immediately after arriving each morning. And, yes, she chanted the letter names as she placed individual pieces on the table in order, and again with the child as the child assembled the pieces. In the early weeks, she gave each child a name card—a duplicate of the puzzle before cutting it up—to place in a "Look Who's Here Today" pocket chart. She started the sign-in chart later. She explained why she no longer used the name puzzles first thing in the morning:

> When puzzle assembly became routine for many children, and they began to just go through the motions, I stopped using them. They are a good starting point, but after a child has learned what they offer, it's better to find authentic ways for children to practice name-writing. I use name puzzles now only as a support in meaningful situations, and with only a few children in a small-group or individual setting. For example, when a child wants to sign a card or put her name on an art project, but cannot recall all letters or their order, I might suggest the name puzzle.

The teacher indicated that she had never used name puzzles in her literacy routines and hadn't thought through the likely length of their usefulness during the summer professional development. She added that she and other teachers usually figured out how something worked when they used a new practice.

The principal suggested finding out about other teachers' experiences with the name puzzles and indicated interest in discussing with all the teachers the commitment to plans agreed on in group professional development. She then summarized the meeting: "Our discussion was about Eliza's unique approach to writing her name and my concerns about it, and about the name puzzles' value as a support." The principal and teacher then agreed to wait a week before insisting that Eliza write the letters in order as they appear in her name. The teacher would watch her sign in and keep notes. A few days later, Eliza did this:

> This is *E*, my letter! My name is Eliza. This is *L*. That's my mommy's letter. Her name is Lisa. This is *I* with a dot. I don't know anyone

who has that letter. This is ziggly-wiggly *Z*. Mommy and me named that one. And this is *A*, for Ali, my friend! *E-L-I-Z-A, ELIZA!*

The same thing happened the next day and each day since.

NO RESOLUTION ABOUT THE MEANING OF ELIZA'S BEHAVIOR

Although Eliza's behavior change had resolved the principal's concern, the disagreement about the meaning of Eliza's unique name-writing approach remained. Without further discussion, the principal and teacher were likely to disagree again about the meaning of other children's behavior. Their different knowledge bases, coupled with different roles in the education setting, were probably at the heart of their different perspectives. The inability of both participants to approach a disagreement analytically also had not helped.

The teacher probably had studied early literacy research and best practices in her graduate program, as well as the importance of play and exploration in preschoolers' learning. In studying early writing, she had probably read about young preschoolers' tendency to view their names' first letter as "theirs" and the first letters in friends' and family members' names similarly.[1] With no inkling yet that letters represent sounds, or that each letter is used in thousands of words, the preschool-age child attributes ownership of first letters to individuals. Eliza's playful twist on this tendency was to "honor" friends and family members' first letters. This behavior probably meshed with the teacher's knowledge of preschoolers' typical behavior, and what she knew about Eliza's social nature and overall personality.

In contrast, the principal focused more narrowly on tasks and results, because she was ultimately responsible for learning schoolwide. Like most principals, her professional library included the Common Core State Standards, her state's and perhaps other states' early-learning standards, and a variety of reports.[2] Her bookshelf probably also held some books about general models of teaching and about teaching literacy, math, and science to young children, although her limited time for reading was likely consumed by standards documents and important reports. Given the principal's lack of detailed knowledge about preschoolers' early literacy knowledge and behavior, her concern about Eliza's "bad habits" was understandable. The challenge for a principal, though, is to figure out whether departing from a more typical way of doing something matters.

Principals are also left adrift when they rely mostly on standards to guide instruction, without bringing underlying knowledge about specific domains of learning to the task. Standards indicate clearly what children at each age level should know and be able to do, but not the specific instruction to support each item in the standards. Standards also do not indicate the path of each item's influence on a specific outcome, such as decoding skill.[3] Name-writing presents exactly this predicament.

WHY NAME-WRITING SKILL IN PREK MIGHT PREDICT DECODING

Name-writing made its way into early-learning writing standards after researchers found that name-writing skill at the end of preK strongly predicts later decoding.[4] The relationship between letter name knowledge and phonological awareness to decoding was obvious: letters represent sounds in spoken words; phonological awareness allows children to detect these sounds. Nothing could be more at the very heart of decoding. In contrast, it was not clear why a preschooler's skill in writing her name should make an additional contribution to later decoding. Although it's always a good idea to unpack a murky predictor before designing instruction, there had been no discussion of this kind in the summer PD before teachers decided to make the name puzzles. The rote instructional approach to name-writing provided by the puzzles might not have matched very well the learning process of children in the studies who had learned to write their names during the preschool years.

What Children Might Learn When Learning to Write Their Names

Perhaps children who write their names learn more letter names, over-all, than children who don't. Or, while writing their names, children might learn to organize print from left to right, which is critical when decoding. Third, name-writing experience could help children develop a higher level of phonological awareness, specifically at the phoneme level, on which alphabetic writing systems are based. Maybe parents or teach-ers explain that *B* is used to write Brian, because *B* makes the /b/ sound, cutting right to the chase, while phonological awareness programs used in preK typically take a more protracted, lockstep approach, and rarely combine phonological awareness training with print. Or perhaps chil-dren figure out sound-letter connections when they notice the first let-ters and first sounds in names of close friends or family members. "Hmm . . . ," a child might think. "Blake's name also starts with *B*, and I wonder why, because it's my letter." Then the light might dawn, with the child noticing that Brian and Blake begin with the same sound. A child might think, "Maybe, that's why *B* is Blake's letter, too!"

Fourth, in decoding, each individual literacy skill is not deployed separately. Instead, to use literacy skills productively to read or write, children must understand how the pieces work together. Learning to write their names provides a context for integrating individual literacy skills. Maybe it's this process that makes name-writing a good predictor of later decoding skill. Although Eliza's teacher could have stressed the sounds in Eliza's name and linked one or more to specific letters (i.e., "We use the letter *Z* for the /z/ sound"), but she had not. Researchers are still trying to figure out what emergent literacy skills preschoolers learn from name-writing, and it seems to depend on the quality of the teach-er's interactions with children in the writing context.[5]

Returning to the Name Puzzle with Eliza

While the principal thought that asking Eliza to use the name puzzle again would change her behavior, Eliza had social and play reasons for her approach to writing her name, and it always ended up correctly, as

ELIZA. If instruction provided with the name puzzle did not give her a good reason to believe her approach was not just as good as anyone else's, she probably wouldn't have changed it.

The teacher's decision to share information about Eliza's early use of the correct sequence in writing the letters in her name, both at home and at school, implied that she thought the correct sequence of letters, once learned, would remain in Eliza's mind. It probably would have, especially if reinforced by seeing her name in multiple locations in preK (e.g., cubby, helpers chart, snack table), because the brain stores letter sequence information from words seen frequently and stores abstract information about common letter sequences in English syllables. This visual knowledge provides strong support for remembering the order of letters in words when writing or reading them.[6]

Possible Benefits to What Eliza Was Doing

Eliza was obviously remembering the letters and their order in her name because she always put the letters she had skipped over in the correct place to create *ELIZA*. She seemed to have a good image in her mind to guide her, and she also had early name-writing experience that focused on both the letters and their order. How otherwise would she have been able to put the missing letters where they belonged?

Playing around, as Eliza did, would likely have prompted important questions and discoveries in the long run. At age four, she knew that some first letters in the names of friends and family members were also in her name, but not why. But later, when beginning to get some inkling that letters in names are related to sounds in their spoken counterparts, Eliza might have taken a closer look and then started piecing together important literacy skills information. For example, she might notice that the *A* in her name is linked to a different sound than the *A* in her friend Ali's name, while *L* in her name and her mother's is linked to the same sound. And maybe Eliza would realize that all three letters in Ali's name are also in hers, and that *i* in Ali represents a different sound than *i* in Eliza. These sophisticated understandings about letters and their function in words, not the bare-bones basics of letter name knowledge and phono-logical awareness, are what set children apart in their later achievement.[7]

IMPLICATIONS FOR INSTRUCTIONAL LEADERS

Eliza had indeed paid close attention to instruction that both her mother and teacher provided. Then, as is common among many young children, she varied her name-writing approach after having mastered it, making it serve a social function and perhaps the daily routine of signing in less mundane. Her behavior indicated cognitive power and attentiveness to instruction, not disregard for what she had learned from her name puzzle.

Instructional leaders must treat standards as a starting point for developing instruction, not the end, and realize that good instruction requires deep understanding of each domain addressed in standards, combined with an understanding of preschoolers' approach to learning, including their tendency to play with learning. It is not helpful to allocate some time and specific activities in the preK day to play and then ban it from academic skills teaching and learning, as the principal suggested when saying, "Isn't name-writing something to just do in a certain way?" There are benefits to experimenting and exploring in different ways to achieve the same end, and joy and pride in accomplishments also affect academic achievement.[8] Moreover, preK is not too early to address the transferable knowledge and skills defined by the Committee for Defining Deeper Learning and 21st Century Skills. Eliza's behavior is an example of creativity in the cognitive domain, specifically, innovation.[9]

PART III

Preschoolers Learn Literacy and Language Skills

PreK teachers probably spend more time discussing, planning, and preparing for literacy skills and oral language instruction than they spend on other early-learning domains, and literacy and language experiences are often prominent in the daily schedule. PreK children typically hear a story read aloud daily and are engaged in a few literacy skills tasks during Circle Time. At Center Time, preK teachers offer writing and book centers, place literacy-related props in the dramatic play and block areas, offer literacy skills materials among the items in the puzzles and manipulatives area, and include alphabet letter stamps in printing supplies at the art table. PreK teachers are also urged to talk with children about block buildings, paintings, drawings, and their discoveries at the water table, and to use the names of various items in conversations as they work and play with children.

In preK state standards, some of the basic literacy skills are included in the list of foundational skills for reading; others are listed in the language standards, as conventions of Standard English; still others are in the writing standards. The basic literacy skills include letter-name knowledge, the ability to detect sounds in spoken words (i.e., phonological awareness), and print conventions (e.g., left to right organization of print). If instructional contexts integrate skills, such as when adults help spell words that children request, preschoolers also acquire the understanding that letters represent sounds in spoken words (i.e., the alphabetic principle) and learn some sound-letter correspondences. Some older preschoolers also begin to notice, from adults' demonstrations and explanations, when helping with spelling, that the letter used to represent a sound often has that sound in its name (e.g., *B* contains /b/; *K* contains /k/) and begin to use this information to invent spellings (e.g., BK for *book*; KD for *candy*).

This attention to literacy skills and language is based on research that shows a strong relationship between children's literacy skill and oral language development in the early years and later reading achievement. For example, in one study, only about 25 percent of the children who struggled to read in first grade were reading at grade level by fourth grade, and these children were the ones who had higher levels of phonological awareness and oral vocabulary when entering first grade than children whose reading skill remained well below the grade level average. They also had several behavioral skills that are related to learning (e.g., paying attention, listening, following directions).[1] Additional information about early literacy and language skills and later success in reading has come from studies that followed children from preK or kindergarten as far as fourth grade.[2] These studies showed that literacy skills acquired by the end of preK are the strongest predictor of a child's success in learning to read (i.e., decoding or word recognition), while oral language, content knowledge, and reasoning have a major impact on their comprehension of challenging texts, starting in third and fourth grade.

Given the weight of the evidence, it is no wonder that preK programs, especially those serving lower-income children, spend so much time on early language and literacy skills instruction. Literacy skills instruction in some preK classrooms sometimes consumes so much time that other important learning is neglected. We are concerned about the amount of time that some preschoolers spend in whole-group, teacher-directed, literacy skills instruction; the instructional strategies used in some preK classrooms; how books are read during story time; and how teachers talk with children about their drawings or when helping children spell words. Too often, literacy skills instruction focuses mostly on bits and pieces, with instruction that is repetitive and rote, and is completely removed from meaningful contexts of use. Books are sometimes read mostly to support oral vocabulary and overall oral language development in ways that compromise listening comprehension, thinking, and children's enjoyment of stories. Conversations with individual children are often short, full of effusive praise, and devoid of substance. Over the years, we've seen preschoolers wiggle, wince, clench their teeth, and sometimes close their eyes and put their fingers in their ears, trying as best as they can to sit through a boring book reading or an altogether too basic and repetitive literacy skills lesson.

Addressing literacy skills and oral language development differently can help children learn more in less time, with greater interest and engagement. Teaching literacy skills and oral language differently requires a view of preschoolers as capable thinkers, which research shows they are, and teachers who are skilled at scaffolding children's thinking and providing feedback. The four chapters in part III illustrate what teachers might do to support children in acquiring literacy skills, oral language, and thinking. Of the four chapters in this part, two address literacy skills instruction, and two focus on oral language, including listening comprehension.

Chapter 9 focuses on letter identification and phonological awareness (PA), using two tasks in tandem, with the result that children learned much more than letter names and sensitivity to first sounds in their names. Readers will see some of the benefits of using instruction that integrates literacy skills, rather than instruction that always addresses each skill separately. Chapter 10 describes basic literacy skills development, using the case of one child who learned these mostly at home. This case also shows how older preschool-age children often develop a strategy for inventing spellings and discusses how experiences influence a child's ideas about spelling. This chapter also illustrates how a children's mind-set about learning—whether they think talent or effort matters most—can affect even young children's motivation to engage in school tasks.

Chapter 11 takes up the topic of how to engage preschoolers in one-on-one conversations during Center Time, and discusses the benefits of one-on-one conservations to preschoolers' language development, cognitive development, and social-emotional well-being. Chapter 12 focuses on higher-level thinking in the story reading context, and the need for teachers to find a balance in this context between supporting oral vocabulary and expressive language, and listening comprehension. The chapter also addresses the reluctance of some preK teachers to guide children's thinking in the story reading context, as well as the difficulty that many preK teachers have in recognizing when young children are thinking, which is most of the time!

CHAPTER 9

Are you a J or a G?

Meeting Standards, and More

WHEN I (JUDY) ARRIVED IN THE CLASSROOM, Center Time had just started. After a quick hello and the teacher's announcement that "Miss Judy is visiting with us today," I headed to the writing center. But before I could sit down, Ginny approached with her question. Thinking I had misheard her words, I asked her to repeat it. Though certain this time of what she had said, I remained puzzled. I glanced across the room to catch the teacher's eye. She knew exactly what to tell me: "Ginny wants to know if your name starts with a *J* or *G*." I told Ginny that "Judy begins with *J*." She said "Okay," very matter of factly and then returned to her friends in the playhouse.

A few weeks later, when visiting another classroom, a child asked, "Do you know my name is Shantelle and it begins with two letters?" With a tone indicating some surprise, I asked, "Which two?" Shantelle answered quickly, with authority: "*S* and *H*!" I told her this made sense, because her name started with /sh/ and *s* and *h* together write this sound. After she said, "I knoooow," I commented how lucky she was to have a name starting with two letters, because most children's names use only one letter to write its first sound. She beamed.

Of the many things a four-year-old might have shared (e.g., "I cutted my finger and got a Band-Aid." "I feeded the fish."), Shantelle had chosen this. During the next few years, I heard similar stories. In thirty-five years of working with preschoolers, I had never heard comments like these. Children sometimes said, "*B* is my letter and *L* is Lydia's," but never anything about different letters representing the same sound or two letters together representing one.

HOW GINNY AND SHANTELLE ACQUIRED THIS KNOWLEDGE

Ginny and Shantelle participated daily in a twenty-minute, whole-group Circle Time, in which their teachers tucked a few literacy tasks among the songs, poems, and games they had used for years. Two of these tasks, used in tandem, created the context in which Ginny and Shantelle learned that some sounds have more than one acceptable spelling, depending on their contexts in a word (e.g., Ginny/Jason) and that other sounds are represented with two letters together. One task focused on first letters in children's names, the second on their first sounds. When implementing the letters task, a teacher showed one letter at a time from a set of alphabet cards, and children raised their hand when the first letter of their name was displayed. For the second task, the teacher said one sound at a time, and children raised a hand when it was the first sound in their name.

Teachers used the letter task for a couple of weeks before introducing the sound task. Once both were in play, they used each one, once or twice a week, on different days, and continued for several months. During the first few weeks, when children sometimes did not respond to their first letter, teachers pulled the child's name card from a prepared set, saying, for example, "Brittany, your name begins with the letter *B* (*points to*) just like Ben's. You may raise your hand now." Similarly, if a child did not respond to his first sound, the teacher might say, "Damon, your name starts with /d/, /d/-amon. You may raise your hand now."

When Ginny's teacher first used the sounds task, Ginny told Jason to put his hand down, because "*G* is my letter, not yours!" She and Jason had held up their hands for different letters in the first letters task, and Ginny just assumed they would hold their hands up at different times in the sounds task. In response to Ginny's misunderstanding, the teacher presented /j/ again, pronounced each child's name, and emphasized its first sound. Ginny agreed that Jason's name started with the same sound as hers. Thereafter, she wondered how other people whose names started with /j/ spelled theirs. She had heard my name in her teacher's announcement and included me in her survey.

Shantelle learned that her name started with two letters, not one, because Shantelle's teacher had added the *sh* digraph to the alphabet card deck. For this situation, her teacher said, "If your name starts with the two letters, *S* and *H*, raise your hand." Shantelle considered her name quite special, because most classmates' names used just one letter.

Digraphs Were Not in the Original Plan

When developing literacy skills tasks in 2003 for a whole-group context—the curriculum used by Ginny's school—I used state early-learning standards and early literacy research as guides. The goal for the letter task was to develop letter-name knowledge; for the sound task, to advance phonological awareness. I had three additional goals for the two tasks, considered together: (1) promote children's understanding that letters in words represent sounds in spoken words (i.e., the "alphabetic principle"), (2) develop some sound-letter association knowledge, and (3) provide situations in which children might notice that a letter's name often contains the sound it spells. Even though these last three goals were not supported explicitly by either task alone, I knew children would probably go beyond the information given and connect specific letters to specific sounds.[1] I also thought some teachers would support children's sound-letter connections learning while helping children spell words they requested at the writing center. For example, if a child requested *rainbow*, a teacher might say, "The /r/ sound is at the beginning of Rafael's name, /r/-Rafael. What letter does he use to write /r/?" The teacher might proceed similarly with /n/ using Nadia's name, and with /b/, using Ben's.

I had thought that children would learn the specific sound-letter connections in their own names and in classmates', but hadn't considered the possibility of some big ideas about English spelling, such as that some sounds have more than one acceptable spelling depending on the word (e.g., kitten/cat; Frederica/Phillip), or that some letters are acceptable spellings for more than one sound (e.g., candy/city; giraffe/gate). And, with my mind on alphabet letter names, as stipulated in state early learning standards, I had not even thought about adding digraphs to the alphabet card sets. A reading specialist brought digraphs to my attention during a discussion and pointed out a potential problem if these were not included in the alphabet card sets:

> What if a child named Shelley or one named Charles or Theo is in the class? If a teacher uses *S* alone for Shelly in the first letter task, and Shelly and classmates learn also that /sh/ is her name's first sound, they might later approach *s* in *sh* (e.g., shoe, ship, sheep, she) as if it were a single *s*, such as in soap, sand, and sun, and translate it into /s/. They would also translate *h* that follows *s* in *sh* as a single letter. Better to provide correct information from the start. Preschoolers won't have trouble treating *s* and *h* as a unit and linking it to the sound /sh/.

This information was consistent with research indicating that children observe letter sequences in words, that the frequency of observing a specific relationship determines its strength in the child's brain, and that this affects a child's response to a letter sequence, such as *sh*, in other words.[2] In our next meeting at the school, I explained my omission to teachers and suggested they add digraphs to their alphabet card sets, if children's names required it. Some teachers, including Shantelle's, embraced the suggestion. Others did not.

Literacy Skills Instruction and Developmentally Appropriate Practice

Hesitation in dealing with print in preschool has a long history. In 2003–2004, the idea of helping preschoolers learn letter names and sound-letter correspondences in a whole-group context was very new. Position statements about developmentally appropriate practices (DAP) for preK had urged teachers to help preschoolers learn about the many uses of reading and writing before teaching letters and sounds formally, in isolation. To support phonological awareness (PA), according to the NAEYC statements, teachers should sing songs and recite poems to expose children to rhyme and alliteration. Although a DAP document published in 2000 focused specifically on learning to read and write and also urged preK teachers to say words slowly to isolate their sounds when children ask for spellings at the writing center, it had not changed preK practices to any extent.[3]

When writing *More Than the ABCs*, published by NAEYC in 1986, I was asked to remove alphabet information. In a 1999 revision of the book, alphabet material was allowed, but only if authentic contexts were stressed. I included discussions about teaching letters in the exploring writing chapter and a chapter about organizing the environment to support literacy skills. To encourage a more open mind about alphabet letters in preK, I stated that "it is only when alphabet teaching takes place in a narrow, linear, 'skills first' program that children find learning about the alphabet tedious and meaningless." The third edition of this book, published in 2013, included a separate chapter devoted to literacy skills.[4] In the meantime, well-intentioned early educators who noticed my name tag at conferences often expressed their alarm. One older woman shook her finger and said, "My dear young lady, you have opened a can of worms with that book!"

In meaningful contexts, preK teachers sometimes encountered complex spelling situations. For example, if helping with *ship*, a teacher might say, "We need both *s* and *h* together to write /sh/." If helping with *bird*, a teacher might say, "We hear the /r/ sound after /b/, but there is an *i* before *r*, even though we don't hear a sound when saying *bird*." In practice, though, most preK teachers isolated only the most salient sounds and those with simple single-letter spellings (e.g., /b/ and /d/ in *bird*) and just dictated the other letters in the words without any explanation. Most preK teachers no doubt dictated *s-h* or *c-h* in words, such as *sheep* or *chipmunk*, without linking these to a sound; still other preK teachers just told children the letters needed to spell a word, thinking it was enough for them to learn some letter names as they were exposed to the idea that letters are used to write words. In their minds, sound-letter connection learning was for kindergarten and first grade, not preK.

A few teachers did try to make the most of authentic contexts, but had too little time to work individually with children. PreK teachers are always outnumbered by at least ten to one, sometimes more. As the importance of literacy skills for a child's later success in learning to read became better understood, some teachers sought ways to do more. As one teacher said:

> The letters in alphabet puzzles and letter-matching materials don't say, "Hey, hi. My name is A," but when I'm in the puzzles and manipulatives area naming letters as children play, I can't get to the writing center, and the assisting teacher can't either. Some children learn literacy skills at home, but many of my children don't. I think I should use a whole-group context to provide more exposure to letters and sound-letter connections.

I had reached the same conclusion, but knew the history of aversion to approaching letters in a formal and isolated way. I thought using children's names might make literacy skills instruction more palatable and would integrate literacy skills, which avoided rote memory approaches to learning (e.g., *b* makes the /b/ sound, *s* the /s/ sound, *y* the /y/ sound) that violated DAP's stress on meaningfulness. But it soon became apparent that some teachers viewed the two tasks, used in tandem, as formal and isolated phonics lessons, another example of pushing kindergarten and first grade down to preK. A few teachers said they would not even use the first-sounds task because the variations that could arise would confuse preschoolers.

Before state early learning standards and the No Child Left Behind Act (NCLB), preK teachers based practice on their beliefs. Kindergarten and the early primary grades changed in the NCLB era, and principals in elementary schools became more aware of research indicating that children were more likely to succeed in reading if they entered kindergarten with letter knowledge and PA. Early Reading First (ERF), a small program funded to promote preK centers of excellence, affected preK directly, with its focus on letter-name knowledge, PA, and oral vocabulary development. It was the ERF context that prompted my work on literacy skills instruction for the whole-group context because proposal guidelines required a whole-group context for some of it.

TEACHERS' QUESTIONS ABOUT THE TWO NEW TASKS

When I had worked with preK teachers, they asked many questions. I discuss four here: (1) Does exposure to many letters at once overwhelm and confuse preschoolers? (2) What about letters that are not the first in any child's name? Should we teach those? (3) Does writing letters help children learn letter shapes and names? (4) Won't my children do poorly on our current letter-name and sound assessments?

During professional development sessions with preK teachers, I explained that exposure to many letters is helpful because it addresses the young child's misconception that small differences among letters can be ignored. Preschoolers have this misconception because most items in categories they experience daily differ a lot. For example, cars are large and small, sedan or SUV, and come in many colors. Yet, all have four wheels, enclosed front and back areas, a steering wheel, a windshield, headlights and taillights, a motor, and doors that open and close. Babies as young as four months can abstract the common features that define the essence of each kind of thing (e.g., cars, dogs, cats, horses) and ignore irrelevant differences (e.g., long hair or short, spots or solid color, big or small).[5]

Children bring this expectation to letter learning, where *E* and *F*, and *C* and *G* are not different exemplars within a category, but each a distinct category with a unique name. Different fonts are the exemplars of each letter, and they vary only in features that don't move one letter into another's territory (e.g., E, *E*). Three-year-old Sara, who wrote her name, *SARA*, did this one day by omitting a critical feature of *A*—the closed top.

She was upset with a teacher's comments about her very good "As and Hs." Working on a hunch, the teacher engaged Sara the next day with an uppercase alphabet puzzle. From this, she learned that Sara was familiar with S, A, and R, but not H. The teacher named H and explained that it looks like A, except that the tops of Hs are open. "Closing their tops helps people know you have written As, not Hs." From that day on, Sara closed the tops of As, even adding an extra line when the upper ends of an A's sides didn't overlap.

Sara's behavior illustrated how exposure to and active comparison of letters help children distinguish one letter from others, which research backs up.[6] Children do not actively compare letters in programs that introduce one letter each week, nor do they compare letters in the first letter in the names task. The first letter in the names task does, however, expose children to multiple letters, which positions them to compare letters in other contexts, such as when playing a letter clue game or matching letter tiles to letters on a playing board.

In terms of whether to expose children to all twenty-six letters, I answered yes, even though state early-learning standards typically stipulate that children should know only fifteen to twenty upper- and lowercase letters. A child who knows at least fifteen to twenty letters in both forms by the end of preK can learn more letters in the early months of kindergarten, and will likely progress adequately in learning to read, though perhaps with a bit more struggling than classmates who know more. This is a situation in which knowing more letters is better than knowing fewer, but it is also true that experiencing a balanced preK program is better than attending one that focuses narrowly on literacy and math skills, which would probably happen more often if the accountability standards stipulated teaching all twenty-six letters.

In meeting with teachers, I acknowledged that some early literacy experts have suggested writing as a good process for preschoolers to learn to distinguish among letters, but that research has not yet been conducted to test this hypothesis.[7] Visual exposure to letters, and experience in comparing their features, is more effective and less frustrating for preschoolers, given their limited fine motor skills. Many preschoolers are, of course, interested in writing letters, when not required to meet specific standards. Teachers certainly should provide writing centers where children can explore making letters and can model letter formation when children request help and then accept each child's effort and current skill. If pressed by supervisors to include letter-writing experience, teachers can use finger paint on a tabletop, which allows the child to use the large muscle in the upper arm to move and an index finger as a writing tool. The space on the tabletop accommodates the large letters that result. Some children paint letters at the easel, using upper-arm muscles, and they can use those same muscles to write on a large whiteboard using dry-erase markers.

Teachers who were using a letter-of-the-week program asked about their ongoing assessment of letters. Teachers worried that changing to the first letters in the names task and the letter clue game would lower their children's performance early in the year, because letters that come early in the alphabet, which they currently teach first, might not occur as first letters in the children's names. This was an administrative issue, and I urged asking about assessing a random selection of letters based on the first letters in the names task as an alternative.

IMPLICATIONS FOR INSTRUCTIONAL LEADERS

Principals in elementary schools are expected to align instructional goals into a continuum from preK through third grade.[8] If this task is approached as mere list making, the achievement gap probably won't decrease. In research conducted in home contexts, the differences in the extent to which parents provided experiences that helped young children begin to understand how print works (e.g., attain the alphabetic principle) made the difference in the children's achievement, and studies in preK and kindergarten showed that including some conceptually based instruction predicts better achievement.[9]

This chapter illustrates how instruction in a whole-group, teacher-directed context can engage preK children and prompt their thinking if literacy skills are integrated, rather than taught in isolation. It also illustrates that instruction on age-level items can be done in ways that allow children to go beyond the age-level mastery items and begin to develop understandings of what will come later. That might sound a bit pushy until one realizes that many children from families who are economically secure often develop these understandings because their parents provide experiences that illustrate how letters and sounds work together. Ginny and Shantelle were from families with low incomes, and of course, they and classmates developed these understandings, too, when given the opportunity in preK. Instructional leaders should discuss with their preK teachers what their current literacy skills instruction allows the children to learn, and think about whether their children deserve to learn more.

CHAPTER 10

Mom, how do you spell "cat"?

Literacy Skills Development

"I THINK IT STARTS WITH *K*, because it sounds like *K*," Adam said, as he looked down at his notepad where he had written "*KAT*." "But I've seen that word before, and it started with *C*!" I (Judy, Adam's mom) confirmed that it does. Doubt about spelling *cat* with *K* had crept into Adam's mind after he saw several books about big cats in his kindergarten's library. This experience led him to conclude that the letter-name matching strategy he had used for so long to invent spellings was unreliable.

For the remaining six weeks of kindergarten, Adam dictated large portions of the books he created to an adult to write. He explained that, when he wrote words himself, they never looked right. When he entered first grade the next fall, he knew his approach to spelling was faulty, but not why. By late October, as classmates finished writing a second book, Adam avoided writing by continuing to work on his first book's illustrations. The day his teacher insisted he add words and "stop worrying and take some risks," he was upset when he got home. I asked some questions:

Does your teacher criticize your spellings?

No. He doesn't care.

Do you think I or Dad will criticize your spelling?

No, you don't care, either. Nobody cares!

Have you asked for help?

Not anymore. He [the teacher] won't help you fix words 'til you finish writing your story and making the pictures. He says don't worry about it.

ADDRESSING THE PROBLEM

Adam assumed that his classmates knew more than he did about spelling and was probably right, because some were already reading. Adam was not. His kindergarten had provided no reading program, and so far in first grade, the children were expected to learn reading basics by writing books and then reading them. Having concluded from the behavior of adults, at home and at school, that reading and writing are largely self-taught, Adam thought he was just not smart in these areas.

I suggested making a dictionary out of a spiral notebook, and Adam agreed. I sounded out each word he requested and linked each sound to letters, explaining departures from one-sound/one-letter spellings, which occurred often. I wrote the words to speed up entry, knowing we would need a lot of words to deal with the vagaries of English spelling. *Kite* was the first word Adam requested. After matching each of its three sounds to a letter and writing them, I said, "We need *e* at the end." Adam said, "I don't get it." I explained that *e* did not represent the last sound in *kite*, as he was thinking a last letter should. Instead, it's silent. Its job is to tell us that the *i* before *t* says its name. "Oh," he said. "If you don't know about silent *e*, you'd just waste *k-i-t* when you want to spell *kite*. Right?" I agreed.

When Adam requested *kick, kid, excellent,* and *elephant,* I knew he would think their spellings were *KEK, KED, AKCLNT/AKSLNT,* and *ALFNT,* respectively. The long vowel phonemes are in letters' names (e.g., *E*than, *a*corn, *i*ce), and Adam's letter-name matching spelling strategy worked well for those. But there are no good letter-name matches for lax (i.e., soft) vowels, and Adam, like most children who invent spellings, made do with the letter for the tense vowel phoneme that was closest in phonetic features to the lax vowel he wanted to spell.[1] I provided an analogy approach instead, using our last name (Schickedanz) and one grandmother's first name (Frances). I also sounded out *excellent* and *elephant*, emphasizing the lax vowel in their last syllable, which most young spellers fail to detect. I also explained that *ck* can represent /k/ in the middle or at the end of a word; that *ph* is sometimes used to represent /f/; and that some letters, including *l* in *excellent*, are sometimes doubled.

After about six weeks, Adam announced that he no longer needed the dictionary, "because spelling is hard and it's okay to fix mistakes later." He had rejected waiting just a few weeks earlier when he thought his approach to spelling was incorrect and his use of it inept. Knowing now that spelling was complex, learned, and required considerable effort, Adam realized that a beginner's errors did not indicate incompetence—an important realization for dropping the fixed mind-set he had acquired over the previous six months and changing back to a growth mind-set that motivated his future learning.[2]

A LOOK BACK: LITERACY SKILLS ACQUISITION AT HOME

Adam learned basic literacy skills mostly at home. He attended preschool for two years, when three and four years old, but preschools did not provide much, if any, literacy skills instruction in 1984–1985, certainly not a systematic and coherent program. An analysis of Adam's early experiences at home shows how he acquired basic literacy skills, how a misconception about spelling can take hold and then linger, and how adults might prevent this from happening.

How Adam Learned Literacy Skills

Adam's first letter-naming experience was with embossed uppercase letters on a baby-dish rim. After just feeling them for months, he began asking "Dat?" as he touched one letter at a time. This mealtime letter-naming game continued for months. Starting at about two-and-a-half, Adam had a set of magnetic letters on the refrigerator door. At first, he used these letters as fish in a lake he imagined on the floor. When helping to pick them up, I said, "Here's the *B* fish; here's the *F* fish."

Later, when Adam was about three-and-a-half, he sometimes arranged a few magnetic letters in a line and asked, "What word is this?" I answered by sounding out the letter string (e.g., *ABAFDO*); most pronunciations did not sound like a real word. I sometimes used a few letters from a string to create a real word (e.g., *DAB*) and linked the letters to sounds in it: "If we put *D* first, then *A*, and then *B*, we get, /d/-/a/-/b/—*dab*, which means 'a little bit.'" Adam also searched for letters to make his name and asked about the names of family members and friends. I named the letters, helped find them, and often linked some to sounds in the name we were creating. Adam also watched *Sesame Street* several times a week, and each program included alphabet skits. Adam also liked the funny characters and literal, text-picture relationships in *Dr. Seuss's ABC*. We read this book several times a week. He'd take a break from it for a while and then return to it again for several weeks, repeating this cycle for more than a year. He also read this book occasionally by himself after that, having memorized it.[3]

Adam acquired basic phonological awareness (PA) by singing songs, reciting nursery rhymes, and playing rhyming and beginning sound games, often in the car. His PA skill developed further when we spelled names for birthday cards or valentines. For example, for *ROBERT*, I sounded /r/ and said, "We use *R* to write that sound, and *O* comes next." Then, I isolated /b/, and named *B*, before sounding /r/. I wrote an *E* before writing *R*, explaining that it is used even though we don't hear a sound for it when we say *Robert*. To finish, I sounded /t/ and named *T*. From these spelling experiences, Adam acquired the insight that letters represent sounds in spoken words (i.e., the alphabetic principle) and noticed, too, that many letters' names contain the sounds they typically represent (e.g., *B*—/b/; *P*—/p/). This insight leads to a letter-name matching strategy for inventing spellings.[4]

It seems amazing that a preschooler could process data and abstract a general pattern of relationships from adult demonstrations and explanation. It is amazing, but also ordinary. Young preschoolers detect patterns in oral language, rules for forming the past tense of verbs and the plural form of nouns. Adults become aware of this prowess when children misapply rules (e.g., *teached, runned, mouses, foots*). Adults assume that children grow out of extending rules to exceptions. Instead, children learn their way out. How quickly this happens depends on how often a child hears each exception. The higher the frequency, the faster a child learns each word.[5]

Preschoolers can detect patterns in written language when adults make the mental processes involved in reading and writing observable. Some parents and teachers provide many of these "cognitive apprenticeship" opportunities, while others provide very few.[6] Unlike oral language, which children can hear, the mental processes of reading and spelling are not typically on display when adults read and write. Adults often think of the process of learning to read and write as a matter of acquiring various pieces that they think make up these domains, such as letter names and sound-letter associations. They often teach these pieces separately, not through demonstrations and explanations, as they read or write with children.

Practice with pieces has its place. Adam learned letter names as I named them on the rim of his baby dish, and when I picked up the magnetic letters he used as fish. But my demonstrations and explanations of letter use when spelling words provided the cognitive apprenticeships that helped Adam pull individual literacy skills together to invent spellings. Our readings of *Dr. Seuss's ABC* also probably helped, because the text's alliteration demonstrates a letter's use in representing sounds (e.g., "David Donald Doo dreamed a dozen donuts . . .").[7]

Large differences exist in the oral language data available to young children, and these differences matter for the child's oral language development and later reading achievement.[8] Nevertheless, most children learn to talk, unless circumstances are extraordinarily bleak. In contrast, many children stumble with reading, despite seeing print all around, hearing adults read, and seeing them write. The problem is that the underlying processes typically remain hidden.

What Adam Didn't Learn About Print During the Preschool Years

Young children who acquire literacy skills, along with some understanding of their relationships (i.e., letters represent sounds in spoken words), often read by finger-pointing books they have memorized. They also sometimes ask for help in spelling words, and adults sometimes respond with demonstrations and explanations, not by dictating the letters or writing words the child can copy. Finger-point reading and adult-mediated spelling can position older preschoolers and kindergartners to obtain more data about English writing, which, in turn, can prompt children to revise their one-sound/one-letter concept of spelling.

Finger-Point Reading

For a short time, Adam read *Dr. Seuss's ABC* book verbatim, using its illustrations to prompt his recall of the text. He didn't look at the words, and his pace mimicked the adult reader's. In contrast, finger-point reading is slow and plodding, because children scan words closely to link the first sound in each word to its first letter.[9] When finger-point reading, a child sees that *caterpillar* and *carrot* start with *C* not *K*, as a letter-name matching spelling strategy suggests. The finger-point reader learns some conventional sound-letter matches (e.g., *c* not *k* for *carrot*; *d* not *w* for *dog*) and acquires some abstract information about conventional letter sequences. This learning takes places without any intention on the child's part. The child's brain just automatically processes information about letter sequences that are within the five- to six-letter span of a child's eye fixations.[10] Children see other whole words in the environment, such as when parents or teachers underline words in a book title or involve a child in helping to compose a thank-you note or short message in a birthday card. Children use this knowledge when they string letters together to make words, before they begin to spell phonetically (e.g., MAMRTO, TOFLIXT). Research has linked this early knowledge about patterns of letters in words to later skill in learning to read.

Invented spellings, such as *BRD* for *bird* and *SPRMN* for *superman*, are not among the high-probability sequences the brain logs in when the child finger-point reads or looks closely at words in book titles or on street signs. As children acquire this orthographic information from words they see in the environment, in books read to them, or in words adults help them spell, they begin to realize that their spellings don't look right. This prompts them to modify their invented spellings. For example, *EGZ* (i.e., *EGGS*) changes to *EGGZ*; *POLEC* might change to *POLEEC*; and *KRS* might change to *KARS*. Though still far from conventional, these spellings contain more features that the child sees. Most importantly, the child's view of spelling broadens beyond a strict, one-sound/one-letter conception, which prompts the question "Is this right?" Adults should answer it.[11]

As an older four-year-old, Adam could have finger-point read books he had memorized (e.g., *Go Dog Go*, *Dr. Seuss's ABC*, *Goodnight Moon*), but he was more interested in informational books. On occasion, when someone suggested returning to a simple book, he wanted to hear an informational book, not read books he no longer found interesting. Later in first grade, when his goal was to learn to read, he read these simple books and then some Berenstain Bears books, which Adam found more interesting and I found more useful because he had to look at the words and use alphabetic skills to recognize them in a book he had not memorized.

Adult-Scaffolded Spelling

I had sounded words out and linked these sounds to letters, as I described earlier in this chapter, which positioned Adam to use a letter-name matching spelling strategy. But then he spelled independently most of the time at home and in kindergarten, where invented spelling was expected. In the 1980s, his kindergarten and many others provided no systematic literacy skills instruction or guided reading program. Given Adam's independence in spelling, adults' ability to read his words, and the absence of an instructional program in kindergarten and the first semester of first grade, Adam remained in the dark about conventional spelling until we worked together on the dictionary.

IMPLICATIONS FOR PREK LITERACY PRACTICES

When developing preK curricula in 2002, I thought kindergarten literacy practices that had been implemented since the 1980s probably would help children overcome misconceptions developed during the preschool years. But I also thought preK literacy instruction could help children develop an understanding of spelling that is broader than a strict one-sound/one-letter conception. Accomplishing this would require instruction that integrates literacy skills, and this thought inspired the first letter/first sound in the names tasks described in chapter 9. The problem in 2003, however, was that the trend in preK was to support each literacy skill separately. This approach stemmed in part from the list format of new early-learning standards, and from the suggestions for instruction that accompanied them, which almost always focused on one literacy skill at a time. For example, to develop preschoolers' PA, they could break words into syllables or think of words that started with the same sound. They could play with letter stamps or use alphabet cookie cutters with dough to learn about letters.[12] Current approaches to literacy skills instruction still often separate skills.

Barriers to integrating literacy skills instruction have come mostly from a conception about PA. First, was a widely held view that PA is developmental, just like learning to walk and talk. Most programs for PA instruction start with environmental sound discrimination, move next to word blending and segmentation (e.g., *rain-drop*, *tea-cup*, *sun-shine*), and then to syllable blending and segmentation. Onset-rime blending and segmentation are next, with phoneme blending and segmenting addressed last. Comprehensive PA programs can consume an entire year and use tasks that isolate PA skill development from its use in relation to letters.[13] By 2003, research showed that mastery of early PA levels was not necessary before children can benefit from teacher-supported, phoneme-level instruction. Seven years later, a study showed that syllable-level blending and segmenting confused children when they began phoneme-level tasks, and that no background with syllable-level instruction was even needed for children to benefit from appropriately scaffolded onset-rime and phoneme-level instruction.[14]

Warnings from some PA experts about not using print in PA instruction created an additional barrier to integrating literacy skills. The concern was that preK teachers would use rote phonics approaches to teach sound-letter associations (e.g., "*B* makes the /b/ sound; *D* makes the /d/ sound"). Experts are right that these approaches do not support PA development, but experts could suggest appropriate uses of print in tasks that also support PA, such as sounding out the words children want to write and linking these sounds to letters. Apparently, some experts think the risk is too high that phonics approaches will be used, perhaps because preschoolers' knowledge of "letter sounds" are often assessed in a widely used tool that asks children to name letters and then tell what sound each letter makes. Assessments sometimes encourage preK teachers to teach test items directly and perhaps spend less time on developing children's PA.

Early educators also often thought that the sequence of children's mastery of isolated PA tasks, from syllable, to onset-rime, to phoneme levels, should dictate a lockstep approach to instruction. But instruction does not necessarily need to follow developmental sequences rigidly. For example, adults do not speak only in single-word utterances when an infant does, nor do they speak to toddlers only in short, ungrammatical, telegraphic sentences. Instead, they use a range of language, with some matching closely the young child's current language, and some going well beyond it. In this way, adults both adapt to the child's current level and provide data on which the child's further language development depends. A strict, lockstep, stage approach to PA or to oral language development hinders both.

IMPLICATIONS FOR INSTRUCTIONAL LEADERS

This chapter provides detailed information about one child's literacy skills development at home and how some of these experiences allowed him to begin to invent spellings. Thus, the chapter gives an idea of where Ginny and Shantelle's early understanding of the alphabetic principle, gained from their teachers' use of two literacy skills tasks in tandem, might eventually lead them, if teachers also helped by sounding words out when the children requested spellings (which they did). This chapter also explains some of the resistance that instructional leaders might encounter from preK teachers if they suggest that PA instruction need not be lockstep and slow, and separated from any uses of print. When instructional leaders understand this history they are better able to encourage changes.

Purcell-Gates found that many of the lower-income parents she studied started helping their children with literacy skills, or increased their support, after their children were in kindergarten and first grade.[15] More parents today, regardless of income, might already do more at home to help their children learn literacy skills than parents did twenty-five years ago, but providing information about how they might help at home is always a good idea. Instructional leaders should support preK teachers in doing this by helping them establish a lending library of books, some that are alphabet books and some with predictable texts that might lead to finger-point reading; literacy games; suggestions that encourage parents to point out and read environmental print (e.g., street signs, food cartons, tee-shirts) and the titles of books they read-aloud to their children.

CHAPTER 11

That's fantastic! Wow, such
great colors! Beautiful!

One-on-One Conversations

TAMIRA PAINTED THREE WIDE VERTICAL LINES in the middle of the paper, each one a different color. She moved her brush back and forth several times to create each rectangular shape, returning her brush to a paint cup as needed. Above these shapes, Tamira painted a rounded spot with yellow paint, using large circular movements. To its right, she started a red spot, but paused to look at the overlap when her brush entered the yellow paint. Her subsequent circular movements were slower and more circumscribed, suggesting determination to keep red paint out of the yellow.

After adding a blue spot to the right of the red one, Tamira looked again at the red paint overlapping the yellow, and then used a brush full of yellow paint to create a dab in the bottom left corner of her paper. She dabbed six more times, creating a row across her paper. Then she grabbed the red paintbrush, placed it on the yellow spot at the beginning of the row, and stirred. Yellow and red stood out in many portions of the final splotch, while orange was prominent in its middle. Tamira looked at the yellow and orange paint clinging to her red brush's bristles and started to put it back in its cup. Instead she carried it with her to the other side of the easel. There, she eyed the paint cups, each with a brush. When back on her side, she placed the brush beside, not in, the red paint cup in the easel tray. She eyed her painting one last time and then called, "Come look!" to the teacher at the nearby water table.

AN OPPORTUNITY LOST

Before responding, the teacher assured the children she'd come right back. She glanced at Tamira's painting as she approached and commented, "Oh, that's fantastic! Wow! Such great colors! It's just beautiful. Now, please put your name on your painting and hang it up to dry." Immediately after returning to the water table, the teacher asked the children to stop bumping the table, explaining that water was spilling onto the floor. She put sections of newspaper over the puddles already there. Tamira paused to observe the water table scene before putting her painting over a rung of the drying rack and hadn't yet finished draping it when the teacher spoke again: "Okay, Jabari, you've had that funnel long enough. It's Leila's turn."

The teacher's focus on managing the water table left no time to engage meaningfully with Tamira. We cannot know with certainty what Tamira had hoped her teacher would notice about her painting, but from my (Judy) vantage point as an observer, I had some ideas. I saw Tamira look at the accidental overlapping of red and yellow paint and put red paint into one yellow splotch, as if deliberately exploring the results of mixing red and yellow paint. I was surprised at first when she stopped so quickly, but then recalled something the teacher had said when commenting about the day's centers.

The teacher had showed three cups of paint and described each as "bright and new, not yet dirty." She meant that today's paint was new, not carried over from previous days. Following these comments, she instructed children about using each brush: "Use the brush that's in each cup for just that color. If you use brushes in other cups of paint, they'll get all dirty, and if you want red or yellow or blue again, you won't have it." PreK children often forget the one-brush-per-cup rule and use the first brush in hand in all the cups, given that the paint cups' tops are open and allow easy access to another brush. When that happens, colors are no longer distinct after a week's workout. A limited supplies budget does not allow frequent dumping of used paint down the drain.

The teacher didn't mention that colors can become dirty if a brush paints over a different color of paint already on the paper. After Tamira deliberately brushed red paint into a dab of yellow, she seemed to realize that the two additional colors on her red paintbrush's bristles could dull the red paint still in that cup. Perhaps she had hoped the teacher would notice her discovery that mixing red and yellow paint makes orange, that she had stopped experimenting to preserve the bright colors, and that the paintbrush from the red paint was sitting next to its cup, not in it.

APPROACHES TO ONE-ON-ONE CONVERSATIONS

With seven or eight centers open, and eighteen to twenty (or more) four-year-olds in a class, two teachers can't possibly see everything that happens or engage meaningfully with each child who calls out, "Come look!" Even when classrooms are well organized and materials are carefully designed to limit safety hazards (e.g., puddles on the floor), teachers invariably miss some of what each child does. Without knowledge of how a child proceeded in creating a painting, a teacher sometimes settles for a few words of praise, especially when the painting is not a picture with recognizable details on which to base comments.

Two language development researchers who understand the importance of talking with children about their drawings and paintings have suggested that adults "listen to the child's story, rather than ask 'What is it?' or assume you already know."[1] I describe two approaches to implementing this excellent advice.

The "I See . . ." and "Can You Tell Me About . . . ?" Approach

The adult starts by looking at the child's painting and describing parts, and then asks a question about something specific. The child's response begins the conversation, and the teacher then participates in a back-and-forth fashion. Tamira's painting serves as an example of how a conversation might start and then progress:

Teacher. I see that you made big round spots (*points to*) with each color you found at the easel today, and some rectangular shapes (*points to*), too. And, down here, I see a long row of yellow spots. Oh, I see some red in this first one, over here (*points to*), but not in any of the others. Can you tell me about that?

Tamira. I did yellow first and made all of them (*sweeps finger down row*). I did red in this one to get orange, because up here it happened (*points to overlap in spot at top of paper*). But I stopped. It could ruin the colors.

Teacher. What do you mean, colors are ruined? You have yellow, red, and orange, all pretty.

Tamira. No, not there. Here (*points to red cup of paint*). The brush, well, the brush (*picks up brush sitting in paint tray*), it got some yellow and some orange (*points to bristles*). I didn't put it back, because it could make the red dirty.

Teacher. Oh, you thought you might ruin the red paint in the cup, because that brush picked up yellow and orange and that's why you didn't put red paint in any of the other yellow spots?

Tamira. Uh-huh.

Teacher. Oh, I see. Thank-you for remembering to keep the colors clean. You know what? Tomorrow, I could put just two colors out— yellow and red—for you to mix to make orange paint. We need some orange, and I could put what you make in one cup when you finish experimenting. We could use it at the easel sometime. And, maybe, the next day, we could have red and blue paint, and you could see what happens. I could save that color in a cup, too. I know we have extra paint cups in the cupboard.

Tamira. Or, maybe, I could. Well, my idea . . . Well, if I had some brushes, I could put a dirty one in here (*points to the easel tray*) and a new one in here (*points to red paint cup*).

Teacher. Yes, yes, you could. Great solution! I can find more brushes in the storage cabinet for the easel tomorrow, and you could try that approach. You can keep all three colors out if you have extra brushes.

Tamira. Yes, I want three colors.

Teacher. Oh, on second thought, let's put the plastic bucket on the floor under the easel for the dirty brushes. At cleanup, the easel helpers can put all brushes in the bucket and put it in the sink basin just as they usually do. That way, we won't need to wash paint smears off the easel tray. How about that?

Tamira. Okay.

The "Tell Me About Your Picture" Approach

With this approach, the teacher starts by asking a child to "tell me about your picture," and then comments and asks questions, as opportunities arise. The approach is especially helpful when a child's painting is a picture of something, but the identity of individual objects and the meaning of the whole are difficult to discern. A conversation might start and unfold like this:

Teacher. Oh, tell me about your painting.

Child. I saw a horse at a parade. A police was riding it, and he holded ropes in his hands to drive the horse down the street.

Teacher. Oh, a police officer was riding a horse in a parade? Were you close to them?

Child. Kind of, but they had fences so we didn't get in the street.

Teacher. Oh. Sounds like there were metal barricades along the parade route to keep people from getting in the way of the parade. You said the police officer held ropes in his hands. Those are called reins, and reins are usually flat like your belt, and made of leather or something like it. Rope is like thick string, kind of round, not flat. Maybe I can bring a piece from home to show you.

Child. Okay.

Teacher. What about the barn? Did you see a barn at the parade?

Child. No. I saw them in books and we had a play barn and animals in the block area once. And there was a horse. So, I know they live in barns.

Teacher. Oh, yes. I remember that play barn. I guess horses that police officers ride sleep in a barn somewhere in the city, not on a farm. Maybe we can find out.

Child. Find out if people can see them. Me and my brother could go.

Teacher. Yes, your brother is old enough to take you. Maybe we could invite a police officer to our class to talk about the horses, and you and the other children could ask questions.

Child. Yeah. Cool!

This approach also works well when a painting does not appear to be realistic and lacks distinct parts about which the teacher might comment. For example, one teacher thought a child's painting was a meaningless mass of white swirls and polka dots on brown construction paper, but learned that it was a picture of a bad snowstorm: "And I couldn't see my Dad, and was scared, and he yelled 'just go to the light.'" The teacher asked, "Where were you when this happened?" From the child's answer, she learned that the child and his father had gotten out of their truck at the end of their long driveway. With so many snowflakes swirling in the darkness, visibility was low, and the child lost sight of his father and the path to their back door. Luckily, a light was on near the door, and the child could walk toward it. With this information, the teacher had a lot to discuss with the child, including the near-white-out conditions in which she drove home on that snowy afternoon.

THE BENEFITS OF ONE-ON-ONE CONVERSATIONS

Extended conversations have many benefits for young children, but most of these are realized only in one-on-one settings, not when teachers lead a discussion with a large group.[2] The different outcomes are related to children's engagement in the two settings, and probably also to how a conversation develops in each one. For example, in a large group, a topic that the teacher pursues might not interest more than a few children. Those not engaged actively probably stop listening. To maintain everyone's engagement, teachers sometimes try to give turns to each child, but the teacher's turns then become routine (e.g., "Good idea. Who else has an idea about . . . ?"). With the teacher's contribution failing to move the conversation along, and the children often repeating the comments of peers, these conversations become boring and devoid of substantive thinking and rich language. The researchers who found difficulties in large-group settings suggested that providing explanations in this context is far more productive than extended back-and-forth discussion. In contrast, back-and-forth conversations between a teacher and just one child during Center Time work well. Engagement is high because the child is interested in the topic, and the teacher responds thoughtfully to what the child says. The teacher's participation not only models moving a topic forward, but also helps the child comment meaningfully.

Learning from one-on-one conversations is both broad and deep. For example, a teacher's sentences are typically more complex than a preschooler's, which provides a model for a child's grammatical development. When teachers take their turn, they also often recast words children have used incorrectly. For example, after the child said, "a police . . . holded ropes," the teacher, in her turn, used the correct verb form (i.e., "You said the police officer held the ropes") and also repaired the child's grammatical error (i.e., "a police"). The teacher also provided the correct term, "reins," because the child had extended the meaning of "ropes" beyond its conventional limits. A teacher's vocabulary is also typically more sophisticated than a preschooler's (e.g., "solution" for "idea"), includes precise technical terms for the child's descriptions (e.g., "white-out" conditions for "I couldn't see my Dad"; "barricades" for "fences"), and includes idioms (e.g., "on second thought").

One-on-one conversations also provide opportunities for minds to meet, because both parties produce and interpret language, and sometimes add information or say something in a different way after realizing they were not understood. In the hypothetical conversation, Tamira clarified her meaning, using both oral language and gestures, and the teacher modified the idea she had first offered in response to Tamira's idea about experimenting with all three colors. In the horse and barn conversation, the child explained why the barn was in the child's picture, though not in the parade, and he and the teacher both contributed thoughts about finding out where the horses lived.

The behavior of the teachers in the one-on-one conversations is consistent with the "mind-mindedness" stance of some mothers who treat their infants as if they have intentions, desires, and beliefs. When infants of mind-minded mothers were preschoolers, they were more skilled in understanding others' minds than preschoolers whose mothers had not displayed mind-mindedness. Mind-minded mothers also collaborated more with their children during their preschool years than other mothers, and treated their child as if competent.[3]

One-on-one conversations also allow teachers to show genuine interest in children's ideas and their experiences outside of school. Responsive and sensitive interactions between teachers and children in the preK classroom are correlated with a better emotional climate in a classroom, which is a good predictor of better outcomes for children's language, literacy, and social development.[4] One-on-one conversations with caring adults also reduce cortisol levels in children who are under stress. This effect is very consequential today, with so many children experiencing stress and research findings indicating that high cortisol levels have serious negative consequences for the developing brain.[5]

IMPLICATIONS FOR INSTRUCTIONAL LEADERS

Although state early-learning standards for language typically include items that address turn-taking conversations, studies of teacher-child talk in preK classrooms indicate that one-on-one conversations are rare. This is not surprising, given twenty to twenty-four children in a preK class and just two teachers. With these ratios, it's impossible for teachers to engage daily with each child, but instructional leaders can reasonably expect each teacher to engage with three or four children daily. If snack and lunch times are considered, the possibilities increase. For example, a teacher might say, "I saw the picture you painted and hung up on the drying rack. Can you tell me about it?" Or, if focusing on the situation at hand, a teacher might say, "So, you said you make cornbread with your Nana? Are there other foods you help make with her? I know she lives with you at your house."

Instructional leaders might start with a baseline observation of a teacher's current behavior and share the findings. When coaches and I did this, teachers were startled to see so many responses that were just pat praise— "Wow!" "Fantastic!" "Good girl!" "Good boy!" Teachers also had been unaware of just how many opportunities for one-on-one conversations occurred during a single Center Time. Some teachers requested that we return in a few weeks to collect data again. The drop in pat praise and the increase in conversations with at least a few back-and-forth turns were dramatic in most cases.

Some teachers expressed concern that one-on-one conversations at the writing center would leave no time for helping children write labels or writing down their comments. Instructional leaders can remind preK teachers that language and content development have strong effects on later reading comprehension, and that teacher-child relationships and the overall emotional climate in the classroom are also influenced positively by one-on-one conversations. Often, there is time to help a child write a few labels after a conversation or for a teacher to write a short summary of what the child said about the drawing. If not, instructional leaders can remind preK teachers of opportunities to support literacy skills in their daily Circle Time, as described in earlier chapters, which then allows teachers to use a few more situations at the writing center for one-on-one conversations.

Instructional leaders might also find that management issues consume too much of a teacher's time. Helping teachers see the value of solving management issues is important, and instructional leaders might do this by engaging one-on-one with children when they visit a classroom. They will discover more about the content of children's drawings and can discuss findings with the teacher in a follow-up conference. Knowing more about children can motivate teachers to solve management issues. An instructional leader might find out that what at first appeared to be a drawing of a rudimentary letter *O* with the letter *T* leaning against it, was instead "the feather that changed the weather," a line from *Bringing the Rain to Kapiti Plain*, that the teacher had read aloud several days earlier.[6] Another child's drawing, comprised of a solid mass of orange ink covering five vertical black marker lines, with *EXIT* written at the top (copied classroom sign), was "my grandfather's house on fire" (an actual event). Other children explained their drawings as "a gumball machine I want for my birthday," "flowers where my Nana died" (a graveside visit), "me, I'm Batman," and "the worms when I went fishing with grandpa. And a hook."

Many teachers have little idea of what they are missing. Instructional leaders can find out and let them know. Sometimes, finding out changes both leaders and teachers because they see that preschool-age children think and have important things on their minds. It's often a new conception of children, not research facts, that prompts a teacher's willingness to change, and research facts are used better, anyway, when teachers get some idea of what transpires during one-on-one conversations.

CHAPTER 12

The cat might go into the street and they'd get runned over.

Story-Reading Goals

THE CHILDREN WERE ON THE RUG listening to *One Dark Night* for the very first time.[1] As the story starts, Jonathan is staring out his bedroom window at bright flashes of lightning in the sky. Then suddenly he spots eyes below in his dark backyard. As soon as he realizes they are a cat's eyes, he runs downstairs to let it into the house. The cat is carrying a kitten in her mouth and puts it down on the floor. Then, the mother cat runs back outside. Jonathan starts to follow, but his grandfather pulls him back into the house. After reading these pages, the teacher commented that Jonathan's grandfather didn't want him to go outside right now.

"Why not?" a child asked. Rather than explain, the teacher asked, "What are your ideas? Why do you think Jonathan's grandfather didn't want him to go outside?" The first child said, "Because you can't go outside when it's dark." The second said the grandfather might be worried that "a stranger out there could hurt him." The teacher said she hoped not, and then called on a third child who thought the grandfather wanted Jonathan to take care of the kitten. "That is a very good idea," the teacher said. The teacher told the children she would ask for only one more idea before reading more of the story. The fourth child thought the grandfather was worried "because the cat might go into the street and they'd get runned over." The teacher agreed that this "would be awful," and then summed up: "Sounds like there are a lot of good reasons why Grandfather wanted Jonathan to stay in the house."

Despite the thunderstorm setting, not a single child mentioned a storm-related danger to explain the grandfather's action. Only one response was book related (i.e., caring for the kitten). The other three probably were reasons children had heard when adults explained why they could not go outside alone at night or run into the street. As with most plotted narratives, understanding a character's action in this story required an inference based on background knowledge. This group of preschoolers seemed to know very little about thunderstorms.

DISCUSSION ABOUT THE CHILDREN'S RESPONSES

In a conversation, the teacher explained that she hadn't guided the children's thinking for fear that criticism would decrease their willingness to think and share ideas. I (Judy) suggested reducing the odds of this outcome by acknowledging a child's response before prompting additional thinking. For example, a teacher might say, "Oh, yes, you are right. The kitten is wet, cold, and scared, and someone needs to take care of it. But on a stormy night, with lightning and wind outside, there might be other reasons. Does anyone have an idea?" The teacher still thought the children's willingness to think might decrease.

We considered next the possibility of answering the first child's question, rather than throwing it back to the group, to just avoid putting the children on the spot. For example, a teacher might say:

> I think Grandfather knew it wasn't safe outside in the thunderstorm. See these lines (*pointing to illustration*) coming down from the clouds? Those are very hot lightning bolts, and one might hit someone and burn them. The wind sometimes blows hard during a thunderstorm; a big branch could break off a tree and fall on someone. I think Grandfather might have been thinking about these dangers.

The teacher's first concern was that this verbal information would not be effective in helping preschoolers understand lightning. She explained that she had commented today after reading this page, instead of asking questions, because she thought preschoolers might misinterpret the book's language, "Grandfather gently draws him inside," as "drawing" a picture. The teacher said she would think about providing more explanations, but worried that not asking questions might limit children's opportunities to think and talk. Most important to my understanding of the teacher's behavior was learning that her primary goal for story reading was language development. She added that children's incorrect answers did not concern her, because they enjoyed stories without understanding why everything happened. I noted that preschoolers often ask questions in discussions that follow a reading, which suggests they want to understand more. I agreed that storybooks are a very good support for oral vocabulary and expressive language development, but also provide an opportunity to support story comprehension.

FEATURES OF DIALOGIC READING

A dialogic reading approach, somewhat related to the teacher's, was developed and researched extensively, starting in the early 1970s. In this approach, the reader makes sure that children can see the pictures because many objects and actions mentioned in the written text are depicted in illustrations. The reader briefly explains the meanings of unfamiliar words as they are encountered while reading. Immediately after the first reading, the adult asks a series of questions to prompt recall of basic story facts. If children do not perform well with these questions, the reader asks the questions again after subsequent readings. During the second, third, and all other readings over the next several days or weeks, the adult asks the children to describe what is happening in the story on each page, or what a character is saying or doing. The adult often uses and asks about key vocabulary words in questions, and elicits considerable expressive language, but never asks questions requiring an inference.

In studies, books were read to small groups of three to five children in the classroom, or to one child at home by a trained parent. Outcomes of interest were usually expressive language; grammatical skill measured by mean length of utterances (MLU); and receptive and expressive oral vocabulary. Studies found significant oral vocabulary and MLU benefits.[2] The studies did not measure the preschoolers' higher-level comprehension, because preschoolers were thought incapable of drawing the necessary inferences. PreK teachers asked only literal questions, and supported vocabulary and expressive language, not higher-level story comprehension.

Benign Neglect or Negative Consequences?

But what if oral vocabulary and a literal facts-only approach to comprehension undermined the higher-level thinking that is critical to later reading comprehension? This concerned me because some dialogic reading materials suggested that teachers use book illustrations in ways that are not related to the story's main ideas or theme. In one example, the adult reader is urged to ask, "What are Clara and Samson playing with in the sandbox?"[3] We learn from the storybook's written text that Clara tells Samson about her party plans, including a trip that afternoon to buy a piñata, and invites him to come along. He quickly says he will, without checking first with a family member. We can infer from both the written text and the children's facial expressions that Samson and Clara are very good friends, probably live near one another, and play together often. Clara and Samson's conversation could have taken place inside the house while playing with other toys, outside on a swing set, or even at Samson's house.

Might asking children to focus on objects in irrelevant background scenes create difficulties later when children are asked to connect story events over several pages or to identify a story's main idea or theme? I thought it might, based on experience reading stories to preschoolers and asking questions. In dialogic reading classrooms, preschoolers responded strangely when I asked a broad question after reaching the last page in a series related to the question. When answering, they looked on the page exposed (i.e., last in the series) and answered with a literal fact depicted there. In these instances, for example, when reading *Peter's Chair*, I asked, "What do you think Peter might be thinking right now about his blue chair that he sees over there in the room?" A child might answer, "He sees his pink crib." "Yes, Peter does see his crib and knows it has been painted pink. But what might he be thinking about his little blue chair?"[4] Another child might say, "It has a flower on it" or "I think he's hiding behind it," because a flower was stenciled on the end of the crib and Peter was crouching behind it. The problem, though, was that neither fact addressed the question. Although the children tried hard, they apparently were so accustomed to answering literal questions, page by page, that they continued even when it made no sense for the question.

After trying a few times to prompt an appropriate response, I typically answered the question:

> Well, I'm thinking that Peter is thinking about saving his little blue chair from his father's paintbrush. The wallpaper here (*points to*) on this page (*turns back to the previous page*), where Peter's father is painting the high chair, is the same as here (*returns to current page with crib and blue chair*). That tells me that the high chair and Peter's father, and the crib and the little blue chair are all in the same room. He already knows that his old cradle has been painted pink, and that his new baby sister is sleeping in it. Peter must have been very excited to see that his chair was still blue, because the book says he shouted, "They didn't paint that yet!" Maybe Peter will ask his father not to paint the chair, or maybe he has another idea. I'll read more and we can see what happens.

Children in other classrooms with teachers who asked only a few questions in a first reading and used many comments to explain their thinking about story events, including some possible reasons for a character's behavior, tried to answer the broader question, and sometimes did a pretty good job.

Given this experience, an article by two reading comprehension experts caught my attention because they criticized the practice of asking early-grades children questions, page by page, as the children read a book. The experts thought doing this "constrained the children's responses to a fact here and a detail there." They noted that children usually answer literal questions correctly, but that a steady focus on "local issues" likely interferes with the children's ability to develop a broader understanding of the whole story.[5] This was what I had observed when posing broader questions to preschoolers with a history of answering only literal questions, page by page. I wondered whether starting with a facts-only local focus at the preschool level might cause harm. There were few answers, because studies of dialogic reading didn't include children's responses to higher-level questions. There was, however, one rare exception.[6]

This study included two intervention groups, one hearing books read according to a specific dialogic approach; the other, hearing a typical shared-reading approach. Small groups of three to five students listened to a story for fifteen minutes a day over six weeks, while a control group played with toys. Both intervention groups heard the same set of stories, although the typical shared-reading group heard two stories each day, in the time the dialogic reading group was consumed by asking literal questions on every page. The researchers measured three behaviors, listening comprehension, receptive and expressive oral vocabulary, and verbal fluency (i.e., amount of talk when describing a picture). No significant differences were found for receptive or expressive oral vocabulary. The dialogic reading group showed more absolute growth in verbal fluency than the typical shared-reading group, though differences were not statistically significant. On the listening comprehension measure, only the typical shared-reading group did significantly better than the control group.

The researchers' main interest was the larger absolute growth in verbal fluency for the dialogic reading group. Because the intervention had lasted only six weeks, the researchers thought a yearlong program would support considerably more oral language competence and help solve oral language delays that the researchers thought were the major impediment to later skill in comprehension. The significantly better listening comprehension in the typical shared-reading group was not probed in further studies, nor did this finding prompt interest in combining dialogic reading and typical shared reading. The researchers didn't comment at all about the possibility that the model of dialogic reading used might have undermined listening comprehension in that group and perhaps would hinder reading comprehension later. This possibility concerned me.

Change Came from a Different Direction

Other researchers who demonstrated that preschoolers could draw inferences ushered in changes in views about preschoolers' capacity for higher-level thinking.[7] Researchers knew that some elementary school children who had poor reading comprehension had adequate oral vocabulary and decoding skill, but did not think actively while reading. They also knew that teaching comprehension strategies to school-age children increased active thinking and improved comprehension.[8] Putting two and two together, some early literacy experts urged more attention to inferential questions for preschoolers and more modeling of higher-level thinking.[9] Some also criticized the focus in previous research on adult-child book sharing because it paid little attention to preschoolers' understanding, while focusing instead on how long the children versus the teacher held the floor, or how many of the teacher's comments continued the topic (i.e., teacher goes along with child's topic) versus initiating the topic (i.e., teacher changes the topic). In other words, the focus was often on how much the children talked and very little on what they understood about a story.[10]

PRESCHOOLERS CAN THINK, BUT NEED HELP

Preschoolers often draw the wrong inferences because they sometimes miss text information, especially in a first reading. They also sometimes misinterpret illustrations and lack background knowledge.[11] Perhaps because of these difficulties, preschoolers often over-rely on their own experience to understand story events.[12] This is what the children did when answering why the grandfather pulled Jonathan back into the house in my earlier example. Teachers can guide children's thinking and provide the absent background information without discouraging children's thinking. In fact, children sometimes comment more when adults comment more and ask fewer questions when reading a story, and children also pick up information when parents explain what's going on in science museum exhibits.[13]

It's difficult to manage a group of twenty to twenty-four preschoolers when posing higher-level questions, and some children become frustrated with long breaks in the reading while the teacher goes back and forth with the children who are engaging directly with a question. Researchers have documented this problem in large-group settings, as noted in chapter 10. To support preschoolers' higher-level thinking, preK teachers can talk aloud to share their thinking, rather than ask children to answer higher-level questions.[14] For example, after reading the first few pages of *Peter's Chair*, after Peter's mother shushes Peter and reminds him to play more quietly, a teacher can pause and comment:

> Peter's mother is not in the room with Peter and Willie, so she doesn't know that Willie knocked down Peter's block building. She thinks Peter was careless with his blocks, and was not thinking about the new baby. (*Turns back a page.*) But look how carefully Peter held his body away from his block tower while placing his toy crocodile on top. No wonder Peter looks so sad here (*returns to current page and points to Peter's face*). I think his mother hurt his feelings when she said he probably didn't remember the new baby. Let's read more and see what happens next.

Children are more tolerant of breaks for a few questions during a second reading, because they are familiar with the whole story. Still, teachers should guide children in answering, using text information and relevant background knowledge to assist children as necessary. Teachers can also reconstruct much of the story with the children in a third reading and reread only some parts, using prompts, such as "What's happening here?" or "What did Clara decide to do next?" Children's comments, even in a third reading, often reveal some story misunderstandings. Understanding what causes children's thinking to go astray helps when guiding children toward greater clarity.

IMPLICATIONS FOR INSTRUCTIONAL LEADERS

The need to address many different goals is a fact of life for preK teachers. Instructional leaders must now look for a balance in a teacher's story reading between oral language and comprehension support. Book selection becomes even more important when story comprehension, not just oral vocabulary, is a primary goal. The patterned sentences and rhyme and alliteration of predictable textbooks typically do not require higher-level thinking. They support literacy skills goals and are also the books that children can memorize easily and like to pretend to read. Simple stories that portray a character in a series of scenes but have no problem or plot also don't require inferential thinking. Stories with a problem and a plot are the ones that require inferential thinking. Instructional leaders should try to ensure that preK classrooms have a range of books (i.e., predictable text, simple stories, plotted narratives, informational) that meet different goals and encourage their teachers to plan when and how to use each kind to maximize its unique benefits.

Teachers are also likely to need some guidance with questions to ask after they have read a story. They might think they should ask literal questions because preK children can answer them quickly and independently. But it is wise to urge something else instead. For example, at the end of *Peter's Chair*, a teacher might say, "I was very surprised that Peter had a change of mind at the end of the story and gave his little blue chair to Susie. I've been wondering why he changed his mind, and I'm going to think about that more before we read the story again tomorrow. You can think about it too." The next day, the teacher might comment on the page where Peter does not fit into his chair: "Hmm . . . I wonder whether

Peter started changing his mind about keeping his chair, right here, when he found out he was too big to sit in it?"

Over time, children will respond to higher-level questions, especially after a book's second or third reading, though teachers usually must guide the discussion. This is new for many preK teachers, and they might need support in this area in some professional development sessions.

PART IV

Preschoolers Think

Effective teaching at any age level rests on having a good idea of learners' capacity and adequate knowledge of each learning domain that learners are expected to tackle. Underestimating cognitive skill in very young children is easy, no matter the situation, because their misunderstandings are both numerous and obvious. Yet, it is a mistake to think there is little going on inside preschoolers' heads. It is true that they lack the knowledge that guides the older child and adult, and are less likely to consider all relevant information when drawing conclusions or when applying past experiences to new situations. Preschoolers are in transition from learning about concrete objects in the world to learning from both oral and written language sources in contexts where physical referents for objects and events are absent. Preschoolers are also beginning to learn about symbol systems for literacy and numeracy.

In many ways, the preschool period brings a new world to the child. Attending to how preschoolers engage with this new world, especially their misconceptions, is vital when hoping to support their cognitive development. There are many questions, too, such as how much assistance and what kind to provide, and whether errors and incomplete understandings should be left to stand or corrected. If corrected, should a preK teacher do this directly and quickly or with gentle nudging by experiences that present additional information to prompt revisions in their thinking? There are also questions about how much to simplify complex domains of learning.

Are the individual pieces of complex wholes enough for now, or should learning be situated within the whole, as much as possible, during the preschool years?

We again raise these questions and dilemmas for preK curriculum and instruction in this part, though discussed already in previous chapters, to highlight preschoolers' thinking. Each chapter in part IV relates to a chapter in part III. Chapter 13 continues the discussion that began in chapter 12 about preschoolers' thinking in the context of stories. Chapter 14 continues a discussion started in chapter 9 about whether preschoolers should be exposed to many letters at once and clarifies how preschoolers think about the visual features of letters, and how this differs from how they learned to think about the physical features of three-dimensional objects.

Chapter 15 is a follow-up to chapter 10, which chronicled one child's acquisition of early literacy skills and discussed a misconception about English spelling and how to prevent it through designing better literacy skills instruction for preK classrooms. The chapter provides information about two other preschoolers' concepts about word creation (i.e., spelling), and their relationship to specific home and preK experiences. Information about Adam in chapter 10, and about Nate and Olivia in chapter 15, illustrates how experiences affect the child's understanding of print. Together, chapters 10 and 15 make clear that a single path is not necessary for reaching the desired end (i.e., a more complete view of spelling's complexity), though a variety of experiences are. The teacher's task is to understand what a preschooler thinks as he or she acquires word-creation knowledge, and to provide experiences that nudge each child appropriately toward a more accurate view.

All chapters in this book, but perhaps especially those in part IV, deal with pedagogical knowledge, which is "knowledge of the useful forms of representation of ideas, the most powerful analogies, illustration, examples, explanations, and demonstrations—in a word, the ways of representing and formulating the subject that make it comprehensible to others."[1] The sources of pedagogical knowledge come from science, and practice—the knowledge gained over time as a teacher teaches.

CHAPTER 13

I think it's that Gilberto boy.

Responding to Story Misunderstandings

THE TEACHER HAD JUST FINISHED READING the last pages of *The Snowy Day* about Peter going across the hall after breakfast and asking a friend to come outside and play in the snow. The illustrations show Peter and his friend, with backs facing us, surrounded by snowbanks.[1] The teacher asked, "What do you think Peter and his friend might play in the snow today?" The children said they might make smiling snow people and snow angels, as Peter had the day before. When the teacher asked if the children thought Peter and his friend might throw snowballs, several said no, explaining that Peter wasn't old enough yet, the conclusion he had reached the day before, after a big boy's snowball had hit him hard in the chest. The teacher then added something more for the children to ponder: "But maybe he thought he wasn't old enough to play with the big boys, because they throw snowballs so hard. Maybe Peter might think he is old enough today, with a friend his own size and age. What do you think?"

Just then, a child asked, "What's him's friend's name?" The teacher replied that the book said only that Peter called to his friend. It didn't give his name. Another child spoke right up to say, "I think it's that Gilberto boy." The teacher said that maybe Peter's friend's name was Gilberto, and that "it would be fun if it was Gilberto and Peter who went to play in the snow together." Gilberto, the main character in *Gilberto and the Wind*, a story the children had heard several times a few weeks earlier, pretends that Wind is his playmate.[2] The teacher did not ask the child why he thought Gilberto might be Peter's friend, but the child's guess was probably based on the boys' similar sizes, their mutual interest in playing outside, and their need for a playmate. The teacher told me (Judy) later that she had probably mentioned Gilberto's lack of a friend when reading the book, to explain why he pretended to play with Wind.

The child used information provided in this book and a previous one to conclude that Gilberto might be Peter's friend. He also probably used his understanding about friends: children who are friends usually have interests in common and are about the same age. Yet, as so often happens with preschoolers, this child had considered many relevant details, but not all. In this case, the child hadn't considered where Gilberto and Peter lived. Gilberto ran through fields of grass near a barn, played on a pasture gate, and waited under trees for apples to fall. We can infer that he lived in the country. Peter, on the other hand, saw snow on the rooftops of nearby buildings when he woke up, which suggests that he lived on an upper floor in an apartment building. Children also had additional information about Peter from *Whistle for Willie*.[3] When their teacher had read it a few weeks earlier, they saw Peter playing on the sidewalk, walking past a barbershop and two girls jumping rope, and crossing a street with a traffic light. He lived in the city. The stories' different settings make it unlikely that Gilberto lived across the hall in Peter's apartment building, unless he was visiting grandparents or other relatives.

TEACHERS' RESPONSES TO THE GILBERTO INFERENCE

In professional development sessions, I often used this example to prompt a discussion about preschoolers' thinking about stories, and how teachers respond to their misunderstandings. The Gilberto example illustrated not only that preschoolers can and do engage in inferential thinking, but also how teachers often respond with total acceptance, not informative feedback, which was a key component in a tool many of the mentors used in this school to assess the quality of a teacher's instruction.[4] I usually asked teachers first to think through the child's thinking that probably led to the Gilberto conclusion, and then to consider the teacher's response, asking themselves, "Would I have responded in the same way, or differently, and why?"

Most teachers realized that this child's thinking had involved several inferences. First, he had pieced together information about a child from two different books; second, he had combined this information with his understanding of friends. We discussed how the child's teacher's modeling of higher-level thinking when reading books had probably influenced the child's level of thinking. Teachers often gave some examples of this from their own classrooms. For example, one teacher told about a child who had drawn a conclusion about the blue-grayish parts of the snowbanks on an opening page of *The Snowy Day*: "I think they colored it and played in it and then it's done now." The teacher said she had mentioned in the first reading of the story that workers had shoveled the snow into big piles. When she responded to the child, she had that in mind: "Well, maybe they did color the snow like we do at the water table, and then play in it."

We discussed this response, and the teacher said that it might have been a good idea to add that the workers probably wouldn't have had time to color snow and play in it, because there was so much snow to shovel, and that she might have mentioned that the coloring in the snowbanks was dirt and sand the workers' shovels had picked up. Many teachers in the group thought the teacher's first comment was just fine because it recognized that a child had brought his own experience to the book, and encouraged other children to do this. Teachers had learned that bringing experience (i.e., background knowledge) to a book aids comprehension. The teacher reconsidered and said that she felt better about her first comment, although she still thought it would be a good idea to mention some other reason for the color the child had noticed on the piles of snow. She added that she also might have commented when out-side with children on the playground. They often had snow, and debris from the ground got into the snow the children shoveled off the tricycle track. The teacher said that it isn't always necessary to comment about something during the story. If the children's experience is relevant, she thought a teacher could comment then and link the situation back to the book. That was a very good point.

When we returned to the Gilberto inference, the teachers agreed that the chances were slim that Gilberto lived in Peter's apartment building. Yet, despite this consideration, they didn't alter their very positive view of the teacher's response. They thought the child's thinking was excep-tional for a preschooler, and that children would begin to consider more details as they got older. I offered an example of how a teacher might acknowledge the child's thinking, comment that the boys probably would enjoy playing together, and then wonder out loud whether Peter's friend might not be Gilberto, because Gilberto lived in the country and Peter lived in the city.

The teachers did not change their minds, for fear that guiding the child's thinking or sharing their own would discourage the children. These reasons were like those of the teacher who hesitated to guide chil-dren's thinking about the grandfather's decision in *One Dark Night* (see chapter 12). Research reviewed by C. M. Mills suggests otherwise, and the developmental psychologist Paul Harris has discussed these ques-tions in a book about the role of adult explanations in children's learn-ing and thinking.[5]

Harris traces the historical roots of the widely held idea among early educators that providing explanations is not wise, starting with Rous-seau. In Rousseau's view, children understand only what they figure out for themselves and they can become vulnerable to accepting others' opinions, instead of thinking for themselves, when adults provide expla-nations. Harris then discussed how Piaget's ideas continued the "allow children to figure things out for themselves" tradition. Harris then indi-cates that children benefit from adult information and explanations, and provides evidence that children don't accept adult explanations passively and substitute them for their own. Instead, they consider adult explanations, along with their own experience-based conclusions. Harris presents evidence that includes instances of rejection when children think they should not trust the adult's view. Additional examples of teachers' responses to children's story misunderstandings shed further light on children's behavior and how it relates to their teacher's behavior.

PRESCHOOLERS' RESPONSES TO ADULT EXPLANATIONS

Preschoolers sometimes reject adult information and explanations, and sometimes accept them. A few examples I've observed in the story-reading context suggest that preschoolers think about and consider what the adult says, in both cases. These examples also illustrate that teachers do sometimes respond to children's misunderstandings with explanations, but typically when they have judged that a child is dealing with facts, not, in their view, thinking.

Examples of Rejection

The teacher finished reading about the enormous bird pushing the boat full of people in the story *Make Way for Ducklings*, and then commented:[6]

Teacher. Oh, look at the great big swan here!

Child. No, it's an ostrich!

Teacher. Well, they both do have long necks. But this is a swan and it's pushing the boat.

As the teacher resumed reading, the child shook his head no and scrunched up his face, as if thinking, "You are wrong about that. It's an ostrich." This child's idea was probably related to a book the teacher had read a few days earlier. In *Chickens Aren't the Only Ones*, an ostrich is pictured and named, and the text states that the ostrich lays the biggest egg.[7] The teacher pointed out the huge ostrich egg on this page in relation to smaller eggs, such as the hummingbird's. A swan is pictured on one page of the book, though not named, and the teacher had not discussed it either. The child seemed to connect the words "a great big bird" in the teacher's comment with information he had acquired about the ostrich from the informational book. The teacher's brief response had stressed only a feature both birds shared, their long necks. Without information about how they differ and why this was a swan, the child held onto his idea.

Another example of rejection occurred in the story *Rabbits and Raindrops*.[8] As a rainstorm ended, a mother rabbit and her babies looked out from under a hedge at some raindrops splattering off a turtle's shell. The teacher read the text and then pointed to the splattering, while commenting that turtles stay dry because they go inside their shells. Then, a boy said, "That looks like a hole in his shell." To check that she had heard correctly, the teacher asked, "Looks like a hole? Here?" The child said, "Yes," and another child said, "I see the hole!" To this, the teacher replied, "Nope! It's a raindrop splattering up." As she resumed reading, one boy rolled his eyes at the other, as if to say, "What does she know?"

The boys lived in a coastal city in the upper northeast United States. They knew quite a lot about whales, but apparently much less about land turtles. They just assumed that turtles could also eject water. The artist's rendering of the splattering, which resembled a fountain, might also have misled them to think some force from under the shell propelled the splatter. Preschoolers don't yet know that storybook illustrations are works of art and take liberties with reality. Preschoolers also focus on illustrations in a first reading and miss some of the text the adult reads. The adult reader can link written text to illustrations to help preschoolers grasp and then use it to interpret illustrations. For example, after reading this page, a teacher might say, "Oh, I see the raindrops splattering off the turtle's shell (*points too*), just like the words said. The artist who painted these pictures made a very big splatter that looks almost like a fountain. But the words say that it's a raindrop that hit the shell and then broke apart and splattered up."

Examples of Acceptance

With *One Dark Night*, one child thought a kitten was in a backpack on the floor, when it was snuggled instead in Jonathan's bathrobe.[9] The teacher turned back to the page where Jonathan went downstairs to let the mother cat in and pointed out Jonathan's bathrobe. Next, she turned to the page where Grandfather pulled Jonathan back inside, pointing out that Jonathan was still wearing the bathrobe. When she returned to the current page, she said, "Now here Jonathan is with the kitten and is no longer wearing his bathrobe. What did he do with it?" Several children, including the child who had thought the kitten was inside a backpack, said, "Gave it to the kitten." The teacher agreed and then read the text that told about Jonathan doing this.

This child had probably noticed the belt loop, which made the gathered-up bathrobe resemble a backpack. Given the exciting events on pages where Jonathan is wearing his robe (e.g., cat coming inside, kitten left by mother, Jonathan running after the cat), children do not notice the incidental detail of the bathrobe, just as we would hope. Even when the bathrobe becomes important, a teacher probably would not have walked through the previous pages to make the bathrobe's origin clear, instead focusing on the important conclusion Jonathan and his grandparents had drawn: the mother cat probably would not return, and they would need to care for the kitten. But given the child's misunderstanding, the teacher explained what was around the kitten.

A second example of a teacher's use of evidence in addressing a child's misunderstanding occurred during a second reading of *Noisy Nora*, when the teacher and children were discussing how Nora's parents and older sister had searched for her first in the mailbox and shrub outside, and in the trash barrel.[10] A child then called out, as if speaking directly to the characters: "She's in the closet! She's in the closet!" The teacher said, "She is, but they don't know that yet," to which the child replied, "Yes, they do! They saw her come out of there!" The teacher explained that, yes, they had, but not until later in the story. "They don't know that yet, here in the story." In this case, the teacher provided an explanation based on her knowledge that story events remain the same, reading after reading, and that characters never know any more at any point in a story than they did the first time the children heard it. In contrast, the teacher and the children know from a first reading what happens, and why.

Young children sometimes have difficulty distinguishing between or remembering what they know and what someone else knows.[11] At other times, children misunderstand who knows what, because they alone cannot make full use of a book's written text. For example, during a reading of *Corduroy*, a child shouted, "On the escalator," as if answering the night watchman's question to Corduroy (*How did you get upstairs?*) for him. The text says that the night watchman had been on the floor above when the lamp crashed and went down the escalator to find out what happened. This event took place several pages after Corduroy had accidentally stepped onto the escalator that took him to the second-floor furniture department.[12]

Preschoolers must process a lot of information to realize that the night watchman couldn't have known how Corduroy got up to the second floor. First, they must understand the book's language, *the floor above*. Then, they must figure out the spatial relationship between Corduroy and the night watchman. To assist children with this, a teacher can reread *floor above* and then walk the children through the night watchman's location on the third floor in relation to Corduroy's, on the second floor, and then review that the night watchman rode the escalator down one floor. A teacher would also explain that a night watchman walks around the entire store each night and would have known that Corduroy was usually in the toy department on the first floor. A teacher would not provide this explanation in a first reading of *Corduroy*, because it would cause a long break in the story and is not essential for the child's basic understanding. But if a child responds as this child did during a second reading, a teacher might explain in this way why the night watchman didn't know how Corduroy got to the furniture department.

ANALYSIS OF TEACHER REACTIONS

In both the swan and turtle-shell cases, the teacher rejected the child's thinking. Teacher behavior in these cases seems inconsistent with earlier examples of teachers' reluctance to guide children's thinking, for fear of discouraging it. But the situations are consistent, because the rejections occurred when teachers thought the children had not been thinking. In other words, when teachers think a fact is so obvious that no thinking is required, they provide a simple correction and resume reading. In contrast, when teachers think a child has thought about something and has drawn a conclusion, they accept the thinking completely, even when it is flawed due to a lack of background knowledge or insufficient use of information from the book.

Even when it comes to facts, the preschool child is thinking, and a teacher should do more than simply correct the child. For example, in the ostrich-swan misunderstanding, the teacher might have said, "We can get the *Chickens Aren't the Only Ones* book out again this afternoon and compare the swan and ostrich pictures to see how they differ." In the turtle-shell misunderstanding, the teacher might have said, "I'll see if we can find a book about turtles and their shells. As far as I know, turtles don't have blowholes like whales."

Preschoolers are always thinking, but are not as skilled as older children or adults in transferring knowledge from one situation to another because they lack well-developed knowledge frameworks to guide them. Still, their problem is not so much a thinking deficit as a knowledge deficit.[13] Preschoolers are in the process of clustering facts into webs of relationships to build knowledge. When listening to *Gilberto and the Wind* and *The Snowy Day*, most preschoolers do not think, "Oh, Gilberto lives in the country" and "Peter lives in the city," because they have not in the past linked specific characteristics to these settings (e.g., pastures, fields of grass, apple trees to farm and country; apartment buildings, sidewalks, traffic lights to city).

Teachers help children build knowledge when they refer to details about story settings and label these in a comment while reading. Doing this makes it easier to respond to an inference, such as that Gilberto was Peter's friend. As it turns out, preK teachers often calculate the effectiveness of a verbal explanation they might provide and the time it might take to pull out the Gilberto book and show pages. In talking with teachers, it became clear to me that concern about children interpreting their comments as criticism is not all that holds them back, though that concern looms large. Sometimes, they feel it would take too long, and story time would last too long. That's a good point. Sometimes, a teacher can address a misunderstanding from one reading of a book in its next reading, by commenting in various ways.

IMPLICATIONS FOR INSTRUCTIONAL LEADERS

Instructional leaders might, perhaps, underestimate preschoolers' capacity to think. I have considered here only a few examples of story misunderstandings. A reader can learn more about children's thinking in the story-reading and other contexts from additional sources.[14] Instructional leaders can share these resources with teachers and ask them to collect examples of misunderstandings in their class. A discussion of goals for story reading is sometimes needed, because, as indicated in chapter 12, oral language goals, not listening comprehension goals, have dominated in the story-reading context.

The education and training of preK teachers must also be taken into consideration, because, historically, verbal explanations have been discouraged. Instructional leaders can provide counter-evidence, including the value to children's learning when adults indicate the evidence behind conclusions they present, as the teachers did in the examples about the kitten and the bathrobe, and about what Nora's parents knew at certain places in the story. Researchers have found that when adults provide evidence for their conclusions, children begin to do the same.[15]

Another deterrent to explanations in preK is a widely used classroom quality indicator that gives great weight to back-and-forth interaction, and penalizes explanations. It also penalizes simple corrections because they don't promote conceptual understanding.[16] Simple corrections are inadequate and teachers can be helped to provide better feedback. The constraint requiring back-and-forth discussion rather than explanation, however, puts preK teachers in a bind, because it is extremely difficult to conduct back-and-forth discussions with twenty to twenty-four preschoolers. Some middle ground might be found, such as providing explanations in the story-reading context, especially now that the power of this assessment tool to predict later achievement has been questioned.[17]

CHAPTER 14

I know! Your mind sees K.

Alphabet Letter Learning

AFTER LEADING THE CHILDREN IN SINGING "Five Green and Speckled Frogs" at Circle Time, the teacher told the children that he would now teach them a new alphabet letter game.

> In this new game, instead of showing you the first letters in your names on cards, I will write a letter. But I won't write the whole letter all at once. I will show you just one part at a time and ask you to guess what letter you think might be in my mind (*points to temple area*). We'll just begin, and you'll learn by playing.

The teacher started by making a long vertical line in the top portion of a whiteboard. "That's the first clue," he told the children. "Does anyone have an idea?" Kaelin did: "I know!" she said, "your mind sees *K*!" The teacher told Kaelin that he knew what she was thinking, and then demonstrated to explain:

> We do start with a long vertical line when we make *K* (*he draws another long vertical line in the bottom portion of the board*). Then, to finish *K*, we add two diagonal lines, one here (*draws it*) and the other here (*draws it*). *K* was a good guess, Kaelin, but *K* isn't the letter in

my mind, because it doesn't have any diagonal lines. Does anyone have a different idea?

"I think *P*," said Pablo. "You are also right in thinking that we make a long vertical line first when we write *P*," said the teacher, starting one near the *K* on the whiteboard. "Then, we add a second line, which is straight at first (*begins line*), and then curves around right here and goes back to the vertical line (*finishes it*). *P* is a good guess, but it's not the letter in my mind. I think it's time to write a second clue."

Starting at the top of the vertical line already in the top portion of the board, the teacher moved his marker to the right to form a short horizontal line. He asked if anyone wanted to guess now. Two hands went up, and the teacher called on Tyrone first. "*T*," he shouted. "I think I know what you are thinking," the teacher said, "because I've noticed that children sometimes make *T* in a way that might look like this for a little while (*gestures to form on board*). I'll show you what I mean." He drew a vertical line near *K* and *P* at the bottom of the board and explained:

Sometimes, when children make a *T*, they start at the top of this vertical line and make a short horizontal line to the right (*draws this*). Then they go back to the vertical line and make another short horizontal line to the left, like this (*draws it*). But grown-ups use just one horizontal line across the top when they make a *T*. I'll show you how they do it. (*Makes new vertical line, moves marker to the left of the line's top, makes a line to the right, going past the vertical line before stopping.*) That's the way I make a *T*, using just one line across the top. The letter in my mind is not *T*, but I see what you were thinking, Tyrone.

He called on Alex next, who said "*L*." The teacher proceeded as he had with Kaelin, Pablo, and Tyrone, this time writing an *L* at the bottom near the other letters, pointing out its short horizontal line at the bottom of the vertical line in contrast to the line he put at the top as a clue for the letter in his mind. "I see what you are thinking, Alex, because the lines I've put together do look a lot like *L*. Do you see the difference?" (*Points back and forth between letter in progress and* L *just formed.*) Then he added the third clue for the letter in his mind, another short horizontal line that started at the middle of the vertical line and extended to its right. Several children called out "*F*," and the teacher confirmed this guess.

Three days later, *E* was the mystery letter. Of course, children guessed *F* after the teacher added the third clue. He confirmed that the letter on the paper right now was *F*, but said that a different letter was in his mind. After a child guessed *P*, the teacher formed another *F* in the bottom portion of his paper, then drew a line from the end of its top horizontal line to the end of the second horizontal line beneath it, saying, "This is the way that children sometimes make the letter *P*." Then he demonstrated how grown-ups write a *P*, by going through the process he'd used before when Pablo had guessed *P*, when *F* was the mystery letter. The teacher then said that the *F* on his paper would not become *P*, that he had a different letter in mind. Because there was not enough time to ask for more guesses, the teacher added the final clue, a third horizontal line drawn from the bottom of the vertical line, to the right. Several children called out "*E*."

WHAT CHILDREN LEARN FROM THIS GAME

This clue game addresses three things that make distinguishing among letters difficult for preschoolers: (1) letters' shared features; (2) orientation used as a distinctive feature; and (3) preschoolers' interpretation that some lines in letters are continuous when they comprise separate segments. For example, when children attempt to write *E*, they sometimes use one continuous line to form the top of *E*, its left side, and its bottom, and then add a second line in the middle. They see in the teacher's demonstration that *E* comprises four segments. This information comes in handy later when children try to write letters. The clue game works with only some uppercase letters, and does not work for lowercase letters, because most have only two segments. This limitation does not matter, because there are enough letters that do work to get across the big ideas that small differences and orientation are important, and help children realize that many letters have more segments than they had thought from just seeing them already formed. This information makes letter identification and naming proceed more productively, and gives children more to go on when they explore writing letters.

Shared Features Issue

The preschooler's difficulty is not in seeing small differences between or among letters (e.g., *B/P/R*; *N/Z*; *L/T/I*; *E/F*; *W/M*), but rather in knowing they should not ignore them. Preschoolers have learned to focus on similarities and ignore differences when identifying objects in the world that are the same kind of thing. They must ignore the difference between a fork with two prongs and one with three to get to the essence of a fork, but they cannot ignore the one line difference between *F* and *E*. Preschoolers' skill in abstracting common features comes in handy for identifying the same letter across different fonts (e.g., E, E, E, *E*, **E**), but not for distinguishing among letters (e.g., *E* and *F*) and attaching correct names to each one.

The clue game plays with features that some letters share, which is why children come up with so many possibilities, most typically the first letter of their name. The final clue focuses their attention on the one small difference between the mystery letter and others that share its features. The teacher does not just say "no" when a child guesses a letter that is not the one in the teacher's mind. The game's instructional power comes from the comparison of the mystery letter with other letters that share its features. This game is another example of a cognitive apprenticeship, because it makes visible what adults consider when deciding what makes a letter unique.[1]

Orientation Matters with Letters

Letter learning is also difficult for preschoolers because orientation in the three-dimensional world doesn't matter. We speak of a glass or a chair as right side up or upside down, not by using a different name for each orientation. Children can and do see orientation differences among letters (e.g., *W/M; N/Z; b/d*), but ignore them because they have no consequence for identifying objects in the three-dimensional world. The clue game assumes that children will at first ignore orientation, for example, and will think the first two lines formed for the mystery letter *F* is *L*. Indeed, if flipped over, bottom to top, the teacher's design does match *L*. The teacher draws *L* to point out the different position of its horizontal line.

Of course, all letters have a conventional orientation, even when changes in a letter's orientation do not cause confusion about its name. For example, even though *S* is not confused with any other letter when it is reversed, it is considered wrong if oriented to the left. The benefit of establishing a conventional orientation for all letters is to handwriting, because using the same movements to create the first parts of *B*, *P*, and *R*; the horizontal lines in *E*, *F*, and *L*; the curves for the letters *C*, *G*, *O*; and the top part of *S* create motor habits that lead to greater handwriting efficiency.

When preschool-age children write, they continue for a while to orient many letters incorrectly, long after they start orienting *W* and *M* correctly. Perhaps they know that everyone will identify the letter they have written and aren't, of course, the least bit interested in handwriting efficiency. Orientation errors also remain for a while because a motor habit must be established before the child is consistent in getting each letter's orientation correct. One hypothesis about why *J* is often the last letter children learn to orient correctly is that all other asymmetrical letters face to the right (e.g., *L*, *B*, *P*, *K*, *R*, *F*, *E*). Given their capacity to detect patterns, preschoolers probably think *J* looks wrong if not oriented to the right like the others. But after seeing it on many occasions, always facing left, this orientation begins to look correct to them, just as "mice" instead of "mouses" begins to sound correct, after children have heard "mice" many times.

E *Has More Than Two Segments;* T *Has Only Two, Not Three*

Letters are already fully formed on alphabet charts, in alphabet books, and on the cards that preK teachers use in playing games. Occasionally preschoolers see how letters are formed, such as when a teacher writes a thank-you note with the whole group in Circle Time, or writes a label or sentence on a child's picture. In these contexts, however, teachers write letters quickly, because they use time on the most important goals, such as sounding out some words and linking letters to them and focusing on the meaning of the message. These decisions indicate the teacher's good judgment.

In contrast, each segment of a letter is made separately in the letter clue game and is described as a specific kind of line (e.g., vertical, horizontal, diagonal, curved, straight, long, short). Handwriting lessons for preschoolers are inappropriate, because their fine motor skills are not yet well developed, and because visual comparison, not writing letters, is the better approach when letter identification and naming are the goals. Seeing an adult write letters can help preschoolers learn some important details about the segments used to form each letter, which is useful as they choose to experiment with writing letters at the writing center. Children in preK classrooms where teachers use the letter clue game sometimes ask the teacher to show them again how a letter of interest is formed. When they try it, some children even use some of the language the teacher has used (e.g., "a long vertical line first . . .").

RELATED EXPERIENCES

After using the letter clue game multiple times, over several weeks, it is useful to play Bingo in a small group of five or six children, with letters that share features selected for the Bingo boards (e.g., *B/R/P*; *E/F/L/T*; *K/X*; *N/Z*; *C/G*; *D/O/Q*). In preK, a board should have no more than three rows with three items each, to avoid making searching the boards too difficult. The teacher proceeds as with any Bingo game, holding up a card, naming the letter on it, and asking children to look for this letter on their boards. If a child covers *R* with a plastic chip when the letter held up is *K*, the teacher points out the small difference between the letters. This game provides a good review and application of learning from the letter clue game, because children practice distinguishing among highly confusable letters and hear the name of each one repeatedly: "Find *R* on your board; the *R*. Look for the *R*." The Bingo game can also include some highly confusable letters that don't work as mystery letters in the clue game because they have only one or two segments (e.g., *O/Q*; *D/O*; *C/G*; *T/L*).

After children have played the letter clue game many times, they can take turns writing clues for letters in a small-group setting. A medium-sized whiteboard can be used, along with a reference alphabet chart. It should contain ten to twelve suitable uppercase letters preselected by the teacher. Making the segments for each letter on the alphabet chart in a different color helps children locate segments they need for giving clues. A child sits in a chair beside the teacher when taking a turn, and the teacher provides guidance about the order of segments, and so on.

The lines the child forms need not be perfect, but must be recognizable. A teacher can provide hand-over-hand guidance, as necessary, or modify a segment quickly, explaining that this will "help the other children recognize it." Children who write a letter do not also write peers' guesses, because doing this would take too much time and present too difficult a challenge. Ideally, each of four children in the group gets two or three turns giving clues during a small-group session. Some children will even figure out which letters remain as options and begin to guess more quickly as the options narrow. This behavior illustrates again that preschoolers like to think.

LOWERCASE LETTERS

Getting a start on learning lowercase letters is useful for preschoolers, because words in the books they will use in learning to read in kindergarten and first grade use uppercase only for first letters in proper names and words at the beginning of sentences. A child who knows very few lowercase letters will have difficulty learning to read. For many letters (e.g., *Cc, Ff, Oo, Pp, Ss, Tt, Uu, Xx*), the physical resemblance of both upper- and lowercase designs is high and makes it easy to learn the lowercase forms. For the letters that have unique upper- and lowercase forms (*Bb, Dd, Ee, Gg, Hh, Qq*), more learning is required. Many states' early learning standards stipulate that children should know fifteen to twenty lowercase letters by the end of preK. About fourteen are close visually to their uppercase forms. Of course, each child is likely to know a somewhat different set of uppercase letters, and depending on which ones they are, a child might know only ten to twelve from their resemblance to their uppercase forms.

Children can be exposed to lowercase letters in a variety of ways. For example, children's names on name cards at the writing table can have the conventional form on one side (i.e., only first letter capitalized), and all uppercase on the other. Many preschoolers are interested in comparing the two forms and begin to link upper- and lowercase letters. Teachers can also provide alphabet charts at the writing table and on the wall, making sure they are the kind with letter pairs, but without the lines and arrows indicating the order and direction in which to write each segment. Some alphabet books, most especially *Dr. Seuss's ABC*, do a wonderful job of pairing upper- and lowercase forms, and of naming letters in the verses on each page.[2] *Chicka Chicka Boom Boom* is not fully appreciated until the final months of a four-year-old preK year, because its humor requires knowledge of both upper- and lowercase forms.[3] Upper- and lowercase letter-matching applications for tablets are also useful in the last few months of preK, as is playing Bingo, using boards with uppercase letters and calling cards in lowercase, for the teacher to show and name. After some experience with Bingo cards, teachers might design five or six pairs of upper- and lowercase memory game cards, for children's independent play if they wish, during Center Time, or in a small-group time.

IMPLICATIONS FOR INSTRUCTIONAL LEADERS

Alphabet letter learning presents a challenge for teachers and instructional leaders. First, their sheer number makes letter-name learning time consuming. Children need frequent encounters for many months in order to learn at least fifteen to twenty letters in both upper- and lowercase forms, as early-learning standards stipulate. Maintaining children's interest and engagement is impossible when teachers use the same old tasks, week after week, throughout the year. Instructional leaders should find out whether the opportunities their preK teachers use are varied enough to maintain interest and engagement. A second question is whether the opportunities they offer early on help preschoolers overcome their misconceptions about the importance of small differences and orientation. A third question is whether some letter-learning opportunities allow thinking and active comparison of letters. If a teacher uses only a few skill-and-drill approaches daily, perhaps pointing to letters on a large alphabet chart and asking individual children to name them, an instructional leader should discuss other approaches the teacher can add. The challenge is to do justice to letter learning, on the one hand, while not numbing preschoolers' minds and consuming so much time in the process that other equally important learning is squeezed out.

Instructional leaders can also urge preK teachers not to rely on writing to help the children learn to distinguish and name letters, but to provide a writing table where children can explore and experiment. In that context, teachers and instructional leaders should not worry when preschoolers write letters backward, as they often do, sometimes within minutes of having written a letter in its correct orientation. Remember that it must seem odd to a preschooler to worry about a specific orientation with letters that are easily identified regardless of orientation. Preschool-age children do pick up this information if they see letters in their correct orientation on alphabet letter charts, in alphabet books, on alphabet cards teachers use for the "first letter in your name" task, and on name tags posted on a classroom's helpers chart. Over time, no letter will look right to preschoolers unless it is oriented as they have repeatedly seen it. At that point, they often ask for specific help, sometimes complaining that they can't get their *S* to go the right way. A teacher can model and even give a child's hand a gentle nudge to the left. With the first movement in that direction, the child often succeeds with the rest.

CHAPTER 15

You don't know many words, do you?

Different Paths to Learning

AT THE WRITING CENTER, one child drew a circle with several short lines extending from its middle and explained, "A birthday cake for my sister. She's seven, this many." She held up five fingers on one hand, three on the other. The teacher suggested that they check: "Five (*gestured toward fully splayed hand*) . . . six, seven. You don't need this next finger, because it makes eight, one too many. I can help you write Happy Birthday if you want to use this picture as a birthday card." After writing her sister's name on the drawing, the child said, "I don't need Happy Birthday on this, because, see the candles?"

Another child copied friends' names from a set of cards in a caddy on the table. He recognized many because the teacher sometimes held up name cards to dismiss children during transitions, and they were posted daily on the Helpers Chart, which this child always checked. With six jobs (e.g., FEED FISH, WATER PLANTS, SNACK HELPER), twenty children, and names changed daily, the odds were good he'd find his name. A third child, Nate, typically drew pictures and talked about them. Sometimes a teacher wrote a few words to accompany a drawing (e.g., "A big crane I saw"; "My slinky"; "Stairs to our apartment"). Today, Nate was not drawing, but was writing instead (e.g., *ETAET, TATNAA, NATEAT, TNATATE*). At first, the teacher thought he was attempting *NATHANIEL*, his full name, but realized he wasn't when he pointed to a letter string and asked, "What word is this?"

The teacher read *TATNAA*, commenting afterward that maybe this was the name of someone in a different class. Then Nate pointed to *ETAET*, and asked, "What word is this?" After sounding the string, the teacher commented that maybe this wasn't a real name. Looking disappointed, Nate said, "I want real words." The teacher said that if Nate told her the words he wanted, she could sound them out and tell him the letters he needed. But then she realized that this approach could take a lot of time and could hinder her ability to visit nearby centers. "I have another idea, Nate," she said. "I'll be right back."

She returned with *A Gardener's Alphabet* and read a few pages, explaining that the big, bold word on each page was the name of an object or action in the illustration (*ARBOR, BULBS, DIG, SEEDS*).[1] She told Nate that he could copy the words, and she would remind him later what they were, or he could just refer to the book. Soon after Nate got started, the teacher left for the dramatic play area and stayed about ten minutes. Shortly before she returned to the writing center, she saw Nate stop at the take-home box (i.e., a laundry basket with large file folders labeled with children's names) on his way to the block area. As she walked back to the writing center, she stopped to look in Nate's folder. Two words were on his paper, *DIG* and *SEEDS*.

SECOND THOUGHTS TWO MONTHS LATER

On some days, Nate drew pictures at the writing center and told a friend or a teacher about them. A teacher sometimes wrote comments and occasionally dictated letters for words Nate requested. Rarely, if ever, did a teacher sound words out, because Nate didn't seem interested. Often, instead of drawing pictures at the writing center, Nate copied words from books. Unlike several classmates, who like Nate were older four-year-olds or young five-year-olds, Nate never attempted to spell words by sounding them out. With only a few months remaining in the preK year, the teachers hoped Nate would become less dependent on books and a teacher's dictation of letters for words he wanted to write. They thought older preschoolers should develop the understanding that letters represent sounds in spoken words and try to invent spellings.

Nate's comfort with copying words might have come from observing his older sister practice writing words several evenings a week to prepare for a spelling test. A preschooler would likely conclude from observing this behavior that learning to spell requires memorizing each word's letter sequence. Nate's teacher had also unwittingly conveyed the same idea by suggesting that Nate copy words from a book. He had no idea that she had suggested this approach to protect her time, not because this was how she thought children should learn how to spell words.

But now, two months later, Nate's teachers decided they would sound out the words for Nate. To use their time efficiently, they decided to sound out words and link a letter or letters to each one, as Nate observed, and then have him copy the words from their paper. With this approach, the time required for Nate physically to write words did not consume a teacher's time. Nate had been able to write letters quite well since early in the preK year. He had mature fine motor skills, for one thing, and he also wrote letters while at his older sister's homework table. The teachers also added new books to the library and removed others, which they did periodically, this time replacing some books from which Nick had copied words with books that had more text per page.

The second time the teachers used their new approach, two days after the first time, Nate wrote two words without commenting. But after the third, he said, "You don't know many words, do you?" The teacher explained that she did know a lot of words, but was thinking out loud to help Nate learn how spelling works. Looking puzzled, Nate said, "I have enough words now." The next day, Nate went to the block area at the beginning of Center Time. He soon spotted some recently added wooden vehicles, all labeled (e.g., *TAXI, POLICE CAR, FIRE TRUCK*). "Does this say *taxi*," he asked. It did. He took a good look at all of them. Nate also looked more closely than before at the miniature street signs (e.g. *STOP, CAUTION, ONE-WAY*), as he positioned them along the streets he had laid out with blocks.

When Nate visited the writing center the following day, he at first drew with markers, while another child drew with colored pencils. The other child soon announced that the color word printed on her green pencil started with *M*, not *G*. The teacher read "*meadow*" and explained that meadows are sunny, moist places where very healthy grass and flowers have a dark-green color and said that this is probably why this pencil was named meadow. After watching this interaction, Nate took a set of colored pencils from the shelf and got a new piece of paper. But instead of drawing, he looked at the color word on each pencil, guessed what it was, and then checked with a teacher. Nate's guesses were all correct, except for *Indigo* and *Sky blue*, which he had guessed were *blue* and *light blue*, apparently noticing that one pencil had just one word, and the other, two. Interestingly, the *I* in *Indigo* did not indicate that the word was *blue*, nor did the *S* in *Sky* indicate *light*. It seems that Nate had noticed one word on one pencil and two on the other, and then based his guesses on each pencil's colors. This behavior indicated that Nate's copying process was not leading to a code-based understanding of spelling.

TEACHERS WONDERED WHAT TO DO

Nate found opportunities everywhere to copy words, and teachers couldn't seem to nudge him toward thinking about how print works. But, soon, there was a lucky breakthrough. It happened when Nate entered the dramatic play area just as Olivia had decided she needed to shop for dinner items and wanted a list to take to the store. "Get that paper and pencil (*points to on shelf*)," she instructed Nate, in older sibling style. When Nate was ready, Olivia continued in the same style: "Now, write this down. Milk. We need milk, and ice cream, and . . ." Nate interrupted to say that he couldn't write these words, and then Olivia started over. "Okay, listen to me: /m/, *Milk*. Write *M*. Do you hear that? /m/-*milk*. Then *K*. You hear that? *Milk*, /k/." After instructing Nate in the same way for ice cream and animal crackers, and he had written these words, Olivia said, "put some lines for other stuff, because we need to go!" But then she said,

"Oh, wait. I'll do that." She placed a series of short zigzag lines, under Nate's *NML KRKRS* entry.

Nate held the list while Olivia sat on the floor, searching in a box for a purse. When they left the house, Nate still held the list. A teacher approached to say hello and ask where they were going. (She had observed from a short distance and, of course, knew.) After Olivia told her, the teacher asked if they had a list. Nate held it up to show her: "Oh, milk, ice cream (*ICKEM*), animal crackers, and a few more things. Well, have a good time at the store." After this day, Olivia often joined Nate at the writing center and advised him about spellings, using her letter-name matching strategy. If Nate knew a word's conventional spelling and, following Olivia's advice, didn't produce it, he told her what letters were missing and where to find the word in the classroom: "*Fish* has an *i* in the middle. It's on the Helpers Chart (*FEED FISH*)." "*STOP* has an *O* in the middle. There's a stop sign in the block area."

He never isolated the sound for the missing letter to provide evidence for a revision. He just knew from having seen the word. Olivia often said, "Oh, I forgot," suggesting that she knew a letter belonged there. More likely, her omissions were due to phonological awareness that was not yet sufficient to detect every sound in a word. It is interesting that Nate didn't insist on writing words that he already knew how to spell and just tell Olivia not to help. Maybe he was interested in Olivia's sounding-out approach. Or maybe he liked her friendship. Children do things with friends they might not do when alone. Olivia certainly liked to help Nate with words, and they both seemed to enjoy working together.

When Nate was at the writing table and Olivia wasn't, he sometimes tried to spell new words on his own, checking with a teacher afterword when he thought a spelling didn't look right, which was quite often. The teacher indicated what she thought Nate had been thinking and advised about corrections. For *beak*, spelled *BK*, the teacher asked, "Did you know that *beak* has three sounds, /b/, /e/, /k/, but think that *B* spells both /b/ and /e/, because its name has both? I can read it, but *beak* has two more letters, an *E* after *B*, and then *A* after *E*." Nate asked the teacher to write *beak* down for him to see. She did, explaining that *E* and *A* work together to write the middle sound in *beak*. Nate sometimes wrote the needed letter above the place in the word where it belonged; at other times, he wrote the whole word again.

WORD-CREATION PROGRESSION IN PRESCHOOLERS

Children who have access to paper and writing tools often start stringing letters together when they are young four-year-olds, sometimes earlier.[2] Children also ask, "What word is this?" Based on letter patterns they have seen in the environment, they develop a few criteria to guide these word-creation attempts. A word must contain several letters, not just one; and the letters for a word must vary. When the same letter is repeated, it may contain two but never three in succession. If the identical letters are used in more than one string, their order must be varied.[3] Using these rules, a child would consider the strings *HBINHA* and *HBIAHN* suitable for a list of words, while *HHHHBBBB* and *B* would not qualify. When adults sound out letter-string words, children discover that most are not real words, even though the letter patterns preschoolers use have the general features of English spelling that preschoolers have gleaned from words observed.

Children often continue this approach for a while, given that a few strings do sound like real words. But children begin to modify their question, based on the feedback. "What word is this?" is changed to "Is this a word?" In time, children realize that the probability that a string they create is a real word (i.e., sounds like one when an adult reads it) is very low, and they decide it is far more productive to copy words from known sources in the environment or ask adults for the spellings of words about which they are curious.

Nate responded with disappointment at the outcome of his first use of letter strings in preK. It usually takes a few weeks or months for a child to give up on this strategy. Perhaps Nate's disappointment came quickly at preK, because this was not his first try. His parents reported that he often sat at the table when his sister practiced her spelling words or did other homework, and sometimes he wrote letters. His parents did not know whether his older sister ever said something discouraging, because they were not always near the table. But older siblings are sometimes critical and, if said with an air of superiority, her comments that Nate's words were not real could have discouraged him. Nate might have been willing to try again with a preK teacher, just in case his sister had tried intentionally to discourage him. Then he found out that his approach did not yield real words.

I (Judy) don't know what happened with Olivia and Nate after the late winter and early spring of their last year of preK, but I would guess their word-creation development paths differed, given different beginnings, home circumstances, and personalities. Olivia had no older sibling to observe writing words for weekly spelling tests, only a younger brother who consumed a lot of her parents' time. Nate's correction of Olivia's invented spellings probably increased her awareness of letter sequences in English words, and maybe prompted her to look more carefully at words on the Helpers Chart and block area street signs. Nate, on the other hand, might have noticed at some point Olivia's letter-name matching system of spelling.

IMPLICATIONS FOR INSTRUCTIONAL LEADERS

Parents and teachers sometimes worry that allowing children to invent spellings will impede their progress in learning to spell and read. Research indicates that inventing spellings is helpful for both reading and writing, because it supports phonological awareness and the acquisition of many conventional sound-letter matches (e.g., /b/ to *B*; /d/ to *D*; /t/ to *T*). But these same researchers agree that young children benefit from experiences that gradually move their concept of how print works beyond their earliest limited views.[4] As discussed earlier, acquiring more visual information about words begins to broaden the preschooler's view of spelling beyond a strict, one-sound/one-letter view. With this idea in place, children begin to inspect print more carefully and learn even more.[5]

For preschoolers, a teacher provides suitable experiences when underlining the words in the titles of books that are read and matching their speech to the print, rather than just gesturing globally toward the words. Lingering briefly at each word's first letter and pacing the reading to allow children to join in also help, because when children do join in, they get a good look at words and typical letter sequences. Providing word cards at the writing table, such as for aquarium-related items (e.g., tank, penguin, iceberg), are suitable for units of study or special experiences, as are sets of words children can use when making cards or writing notes (e.g., DEAR, LOVE). Road signs in the block area are another opportunity for children to see print, as are puzzles that have words on them. PreK teachers can also use printed words at transitions when dismissing children from a group, using clothing details, such as colors (e.g., "If you are wearing something that has RED on it, you may go to your cubby to get your snack"), patterns (e.g., "If you are wearing something that has STRIPES, you may . . . "), or some other feature (e.g., "If you are wearing something that has POCKETS . . . a ZIPPER . . . ").

Instructional leaders might also support preK, K, and first-grade teachers working together to prepare printed information about invented spelling for parents. This resource would include information about the basic literacy skills that are the foundation for inventing spelling, samples of invented spelling showing how they typically change over time, and descriptions of experiences at each age or grade level that expose children to conventional spellings. A resource such as this not only would benefit parents, but would serve as a vehicle for preK, K, and first-grade teachers to understand better how each of these grades contributes to children's development in this area.

PART V

PreK Change Agents

The first four parts of this book have focused on preschoolers' learning, on some of the learning domains of importance in the early years, and on interactions between the young learner and specific features of these domains. These parts of the book have also dealt with instructional approaches and settings, and the effects of the physical environment on the behavior of both preK teachers and children. We also noted the changes over the past fifty years in views about the processes involved in a child's development, and the effects of these changes on preK programming. We have stressed our concern for narrowly focused "rigor" that underestimates preschoolers' cognitive capacity and might well curtail rather than expand their learning, and the lack of sufficient emphasis in some preK programs on social behavior, broad oral language and content knowledge development, and too many approaches to academic skills that develop "just the facts," without understanding. We have told stories about teachers' successes and failures, and ways that some teachers have worked and learned their way out of a bind, or might have.

Part V provides another look at preK education within the setting of the elementary school. The chapters in this part focus on the principal's leadership in effectively integrating preK classrooms into this setting. Chapter 16 takes up the case of a principal whose prior experiences were in the primary grades and her struggle to come to a common understanding with preK teachers about the role of developmentally appropriate practice and how best to help young students acquire letter-name and letter-sound knowledge within the context of a low-performing preK through third-grade school. Communication between the principal and the preK teachers broke down completely, and the outside coach, provided by the district, who had tried for several months to negotiate disputes, had to devise an intervention that placed the teachers and principal on a level playing field to solve their philosophical differences.

Chapter 17 focuses on a different principal, one with a good understanding of preK curriculum and instruction, but very few resources to support the professional development of teachers, schoolwide. The chapter illustrates how a consultant can be an important resource for a principal in designing and leading professional development that meets the needs of preK teachers, even on a tight budget.

Chapter 18 illustrates how a principal approached the complex task of fully integrating two preK classrooms into a K–fifth-grade school, and engaged a professional development provider as a partner in this process.

CHAPTER 16

What went wrong?

Improving Principal-Teacher Communication

MS. J WAS STARTING HER SECOND YEAR at a small school with classrooms spanning prekindergarten through third grade. Having spent one year adapting to the principal's role, Ms. J wanted to focus next on polishing her communication skills. Guided as much by classroom teaching experience as her principal-preparation program, Ms. J was determined to develop positive relationships and good communication with her teachers. She organized the school schedule to allow teaching teams to meet for ninety minutes weekly during the school day to plan curriculum and discuss instruction, and for the full faculty to meet for one hour, biweekly, to discuss schoolwide business. Teachers also had opportunities for schoolwide after-school, professional development at various schools and the district office, and could choose sessions to meet their needs.

I (Catherine) was the early childhood instructional coach from the district office. When in Ms. J's school each week for one day, I supported teachers and principals, new to the early childhood department, in implementing state standards consistently with developmentally appropriate practice (DAP). That included demonstrating lessons, co-teaching, sometimes leading a professional development meeting, and finding resources.

The general schedule that Ms. J and I developed included her participation in the weekly preK and kindergarten team meetings. Ms. J could not attend either one in its entirety because they met simultaneously.

PRESCHOOL TEAM MEETINGS

Team meetings included lively discussion and debates, and work sessions. The principal and I began attending the preK team meetings jointly after difficulties arose early in the year, when it became apparent that the principal's narrow focus on academics clashed with the preK teachers' commitment to the broader focus of DAP. Indeed, the principal was serious about aligning goals for preK, kindergarten, and the primary grades to support coherent and continuous learning that would prepare children fully for academic work in fourth grade and beyond. PreK teachers were upset that the principal wanted them to teach letter sounds directly and spend more time each day on skills teaching. The preK teachers thought these changes would have detrimental effects on the children's social and physical development.

As the year progressed and tensions built between the preK teachers and the principal, I often negotiated the differing perspectives. But even this effort could not prevent meetings from ending before disputes were resolved. I heard from both parties that discussions often continued beyond the meetings and, if anything, made the situation worse. Without the principal's understanding of DAP, and the preK teachers' understanding of Common Core State Standards and other standards, common ground was always out of reach. By late fall, preK teachers participated differently in meetings when they and I met alone than when the principal joined the conversation. As Ms. J became more directive, preK teachers began to acquiesce in her presence and speak against her views only in her absence. Meetings were tense and contentious.

A Critical Turning Point

During the second week in January, preK teachers started to plan small-group instruction for children whose letter identification and letter-sound knowledge lagged behind their classmates'. Until winter break, teachers had used children's names and several games in a whole-group context to call attention to letters and sounds, and had also modeled the spelling of words while writing with children, making sure to articulate their speech carefully to make each sound distinct and then linking sounds to letters. By late December, most children in the preK classes could identify most alphabet letters and knew the sounds that some letters represent. Others, however, knew far fewer letters and associated sounds than was expected by midyear. PreK teachers used team meetings to discuss how to help these children.

The teachers first considered more of the same, but in small groups. Their concern, though, was that repeating the fall's instruction might bore the children or fail again. The step-by-step approaches provided in some commercial phonics programs were also considered, but preK teachers knew that rote-memory instruction did not develop the understanding that letters represent sounds in spoken words. Without understanding, children could not apply literacy skills to writing or reading. Teachers also considered just following the next lessons in the current curriculum, thinking that more time with it might work. But, if it didn't, they would have deprived children of instruction that was more direct.

I suggested stepping back before adding to the list to consider the research behind the curriculum in use now and each alternative from that perspective. I began by reviewing phonological awareness, an oral language skill related to children's realization that spoken words comprise individual sounds. Children could just memorize "*B* makes the /b/ sound" if given enough practice, but probably couldn't use this information to spell words without experience in seeing a teacher link sounds to letters when writing words.

One teacher added that rote-memory approaches to letter sounds, though expedient for immediate testing, can undermine later assessments that ask children to spell a few simple words. We all agreed that it's unfortunate when a preK assessment of letter-sound knowledge leads teachers and administrators to think that they should just teach letter-sound pairs directly. The teacher then continued: "If preschoolers learn sound-letter relationships through meaningful tasks, and understand how letters are related to sounds in spoken words, then some additional practice on typical letter-sound pairings might help. But I'd need to know what each child understands, before adding direct instruction on letter-sound pairings. To find out, I might . . ."

Ms. J had just joined the meeting, saying, "I don't mean to interrupt. Keep going." But the teacher who had been explaining her opposition to a rote-memory approach alone did not continue. I began to sum up and added a few more points, for example, that phonological awareness is a process of sensitizing children to the sound segments in words and that alphabet letters, whose use in words is related to phonological awareness, involve visual elements at the beginning, because letters must be distinguished from one another. I started to suggest the need to address this aspect of letter learning, but the principal cut in to say, "This is not the time to review development and theories about how children learn early literacy skills. We only have forty-five minutes left today, and I want a written plan for how you will teach each child of concern letter names and the sounds that go along with them."

The teachers became silent. I attempted to explain, for Ms. J's benefit, that what we know about children's learning helps in designing and adjusting instruction. It would be easy to find out whether some children mismatch pairs of closely related letters, for example, E with F, or K with N. If a child's confusion is in differentiating among letters, teachers should address it. For example, if a child thinks B and R are the same letter because they look alike, drilling on "B makes the /b/ sound" would not improve performance on the assessment, because children must identify the letter and then say its sound. If a child says R when the letter is B and responds /r/, that's a different situation. Knowing the details of assessment responses provides more information for follow-up instruction. Ms. J wanted action and said, "Well, I'm sorry. You can waste too much time thinking about why children learn this or that or why they don't. Instead of dwelling on all sorts of excuses for why learning is difficult, I want a plan along with action steps for implementing it!"

I then suggested returning to the options discussed earlier and started writing them on chart paper, to allow teachers to speak to their pros and cons. There was some brief discussion about each one, including a comment by one teacher that perhaps too much is asked of preK children and that instruction was not sufficiently developmentally appropriate for her children. At this point, Ms. J stated emphatically the need for higher expectations for all children, including four year olds from families with few resources, like many in this school. She also suggested that the teachers just needed to believe in the children's capabilities and make tasks more developmentally appropriate by using songs and games, and enthusiasm. She proposed consulting with the kindergarten team and reading specialist about new activities they created for children who have come to them without the alphabet knowledge required for decoding: "If they can get it done in a short time, I think you can do the same during the preK year."

I also recommended that anyone attending a preK-level district professional development offering after school might check with teachers from other schools to find out what they do when some children lag in letter-names and letter-sound knowledge. Teachers planning to attend a session agreed to report back in our next meeting, but the meeting's tone had changed. Rather than positive and talkative, teachers were quiet, as if defeated. Ms. J left quickly after the meeting, and teachers prepared to return to classrooms. As I walked down the hall, a preK teacher apologized for Ms. J's treatment and advised that I not take her comments personally: "She does that to us all the time. She doesn't think we are doing enough, but we consider her approach developmentally inappropriate. I'm not sure even you can help resolve our differences." That comment convinced me that I had to broach the principal-teacher communication problem with the principal in our after-school meeting that day.

Thinking About the Debrief with the Principal

I wondered whether a district meeting about school achievement had urged principals to double-down on making sure all third graders met upper-elementary expectations. Or, maybe Ms. J had concluded from a recent review of schoolwide data that earlier grades should do more to help second and third graders meet benchmarks. Maybe she was frustrated about slow progress in convincing preK teachers to teach more academics and about having to exert more influence. I jotted notes about the preK meeting, primarily the teachers' reliance on using DAP as a guideline for deciding both what to teach and how to teach it, while the principal viewed DAP merely as a way to make learning more fun and palatable (e.g., use music, games, and enthusiasm), not as a filter for decisions about what to teach. Ms. J didn't think about the complexity of what was involved in learning something, only about teaching the end product.

The preK teachers' resistance to Ms. J was not due to differences in what they thought a specific learning domain involved, nor to low expectations. They knew that phonological awareness development is not the same as learning sound associations to letters, because their training focused on this. Elementary trained teachers, in contrast, learn how to teach phonics, and just assume that the phonological awareness (PA) and alphabetic foundations for phonics are there, or aren't even aware of their importance. I also recalled studies of first graders who struggled in learning to read and wondered whether Ms. J knew that the 25 percent who recovered by fourth grade had stronger PA, oral language skills, and social behavior skills than the 75 percent who didn't.[1] The preK teachers also focused on all aspects of development, while the principal focused only on academic learning. I wondered further if Ms. J realized that social skills are strong predictors of long-term academic achievement.[2] PreK teachers read and hear about this repeatedly, because social behavior becomes established early. Preventing social problems is a major takeaway in a preK teacher's early childhood preparation.

The principal-teacher communication problem was further complicated by Ms. J's communication style. Although she did listen to teachers, she was not easily persuaded to adopt perspectives differing from hers. She was demanding and expected action that ensured learning in all children, yet held to a certain view of efficient, effective, and rigorous instruction. Other equally strong and demanding principals were typically more careful about communicating beliefs and demands, which led to more genuine listening. This listening, in turn, led to more understanding of the preK teachers' perspective. Ms. J's approach, on the other hand, cut off the possibility of reaching understanding. She was very familiar with grade-level standards and the Common Core State Standards, but probably had not studied DAP documents and state early-learning standards to any extent.

THE DEBRIEF

The forty-five-minute meeting at the end of the day usually started with a quick summary of my classroom activities and then moved to next steps to support teachers. Meetings also sometimes included discussion of issues that arose in preK and kindergarten meetings. Ms. J commented immediately about the preK team: "What's going on with that preK team? I don't know what to do with them now that they are so oppositional." I suggested she think about the meetings with this team earlier in the year and whether today's meeting was a blip on the screen or typical. Ms. J acknowledged that discussions about what preschoolers should learn, having high expectations for all children, and how teachers should teach had always been tense. She was frank: "It's not my preference for leading, but I do pull rank, because it's the only way to get them to act. Before any meeting ends now, I tell them what I want to see in their classrooms." However, in spite of teachers agreeing or not responding at all at the meeting, when Ms. J visited their classrooms, she often saw compliance with her suggestions, but little enthusiasm or conviction. On the other hand, when she observed preK teachers implementing their own plans, she saw engagement and enthusiasm.

I suggested that the way the principal conveyed her ideas and wishes was more likely the problem. She also indicated that the issues underlying their differences could be at the heart of this communication problem. She shared her belief that discussing DAP and high expectations is important, but that opportunity had been cut off today when she issued a directive, which did little to lead to any understanding of differing views.

The principal asked more about DAP and preK, what constitutes high expectations for preK, and what other strategies she might use to negotiate differences with teachers. I started with DAP and its place in preK teachers' thinking, explaining that DAP is a position statement, now in its third edition, published by NAEYC.[3] Each edition has a theoretical underpinning, which, for the first edition, portrayed readiness as driven primarily by maturation. All academic skills learning was considered inappropriate, because children's oral language was not ready, nor their fine motor skills, and so on. This developmental stance of "wait for readiness" was criticized as outdated, in view of considerable research. The second and third editions considered maturation as having a role in development, but gave experience a critical role. Consideration of all areas of development—the whole child—not just cognition and, especially, not just academic learning remained a hallmark of DAP, because all areas affect one another. NAEYC collaborated with the International Reading Association and the National Council of Teachers of Mathematics on two position statements that focused on academic learning, one each for literacy and math.[4]

Teachers' interpretations of DAP depend on the version they have read and the views of colleagues. Teachers who are familiar with the *Learning to Read and Write* and the *Early Childhood Mathematics* documents have a better grounding in the knowledge base about learning and teaching literacy and math than teachers who have not studied these documents. But, no matter the DAP edition read, most early childhood teachers consider DAP as a bible and often use it as evidence for working with young children. Because DAP stresses all areas of development, not just academics, preK teachers sometimes resist requests to add more academics. DAP also stresses understanding and meaningfulness in learning, along with a consideration of children's interests and their ability to make choices. Understanding secures learning, and interests affect motivation and engagement. Choice making is equally related to interest and motivation, as well as to life in a democracy.

It is also true that teachers who are not up to date sometimes use DAP as a reason just to wait for academic readiness rather than provide experiences to support it. Recently, various professional groups have called for more play in response to programs that have become highly academic. Some preK teachers have jumped on the play bandwagon, fearing that they might lose play in their programs, even though play would not be at risk if they addressed academic skills somewhat more.

DAP is not a perfect document. For one thing, it's biased toward small-group instruction and spontaneous individual teaching, when schools and childcare programs are staffed more for whole-group instruction, at least some of the time. DAP should consider how a preK's whole-group setting might be used for literacy skills instruction in an engaging and thoughtful way. Second, more research is needed to understand the variety of ways that young children learn, not just the ideal, highly interactive, back-and-forth discussions, the interactions that are used as examples in DAP documents and are the most valued in a widely used, early childhood quality assessment.[5] For example, quality explanations with demonstrations or, in a book reading context, good use of the illustrations can work effectively in a whole-group setting. In one study, researchers found that extended conversations in a whole-group setting did not predict later language and literacy skills at the kindergarten level, while one-on-one conversations during Centers Time did. Apparently in a large group, many children just stop attending to extended back-and-forth conversations. The researchers concluded that teacher-directed explanations are preferable in larger group settings and, in fact, do correlate with higher performance on kindergarten assessments.[6] DAP is a good reminder that young children learn differently than their older peers and that all areas of development are interdependent, but it still has limitations.

I expected Ms. J to have questions or to comment about this description of DAP, but instead she said that teachers use "developmentally appropriate" as a knee-jerk reaction when they think something is too hard for their students. She knew that the focus for preK, historically, had been on the whole child, while the emphasis in primary education had been on academic learning. She thought modifications were needed in the whole-child view, given today's educational climate.[7]

I realized that Ms. J would continue to hold her ground and not try to meet the preK teachers halfway. A working session intervention was needed to address the problem. With some academic goals agreed to by the preK team, the group could work together to figure out how to meet the goals, taking account of DAP. A special, longer meeting would be necessary to allow reading and discussion of some of the most recent DAP publications and then developing a set of guidelines for addressing academic areas, such as literacy and math, in this school's preK classrooms.

Ms. J agreed to discussing DAP more thoroughly to develop some common ground and thought it was equally important to consider state and district learning standards, as well as both the Common Core State Standards and the Next Generation Science Standards.[8] Her point was that preK teachers needed to understand better what was required in standards for kindergarten and the primary grades, because, without that, they couldn't know what these teachers face. It was a fair and good idea, although too much to tackle in just one meeting. Ms. J asked me to take the lead, because she thought it would not work if she was in that role. We agreed that the purpose of the meeting was to answer the question, "Given examples of realistic expectation for learning outcomes in preK, how can these be achieved in a way that is DAP?" Before the meeting, I had to design the problem set—examples of instruction—for everyone to discuss in terms of both DAP and grade-level standards. And the discussion needed to begin the following week, given that this work would undoubtedly become an extended project.

Planning for the First Meeting

It was my responsibility to design a session that addressed the philosophical differences between the preK teachers and the principal, within the context of current work. Realizing that just continuing the discussion would probably not produce any changes in either party's thinking, I decided to continue with a focus on small-group interventions for children, this time using emergent writing samples.

By midyear, the teachers looked carefully at children's latest writing samples in relation to those from early fall and usually saw some changes. Some children usually had progressed from rudimentary pictures to simple drawings with marks that represented letters or words. Some children were by midyear adding their names or simple labels for pictures. Most children had something to say about their pieces. Some described their drawings (e.g., "This is me and this is my mom. Here's the ball we were throwing."), while others retold an event in story-like fashion (e.g., "One day my mom and me played baseball. I hit the ball so far."). But a few children usually continued with very rudimentary scribbling and had little to say about their drawings. Teachers were interested in supporting children's progress, and this provided an excellent context for discussion of realistic goals and appropriate ways to achieve them, and it gave a reason to refer to DAP publications and standards documents.

First, I established some ground rules: (1) teachers and the principal both had to come to the meeting with some familiarity of the most recent DAP publication and the Common Core State Standards, and use these documents when contributing to the discussion; (2) everyone had to listen to others' perspectives before adding their own and seek clarification before disagreeing; (3) participants had to agree that some diversion away from small-group interventions was okay for the purpose of discussing underlying philosophical differences about the best way to address children's needs. Setting a specific time for diversions and using a timer to make sure time limits were respected was another consideration.

Next, I had to choose some relevant goals for the team, enough so the group could choose two or three to work on. I made a list of several possibilities. For those with children at the scribbling stage, for example, there were the following:

- giving meaning to scribbles by describing the people, objects, or events represented
- noticing how others represent something they want to say
- observing how lines, circles and other shapes can form simple representations

The group would be responsible for figuring out how to address the chosen goals for small groups and making sure that their plans were both DAP and rigorous enough to move children toward the next level of expectations stipulated in the standards. While choosing the right goal for each child would involve consideration of the child's previous experiences with writing, teachers could develop an action plan for several children in the classroom and differentiate for individuals. I tabbed the research section of the Joint NAEYC/IRA Position Statement and the Knowledge of Print section of *Learning to Read & Write* to make it easier for teachers to use these documents during the meeting, and I made copies of the preK, kindergarten, and first-grade writing standards from the state's curriculum frameworks for literacy to give teachers a chance to see what was ahead for the children, even though I thought the anchor standards might be too general for the task.

As the facilitator, I had to pay careful attention to how the conversation proceeded, and to its content. I wanted the preK team and the principal to operate on a level playing field and work toward a common ground. It would take time, but I hoped this meeting would be the first of several that would be structured similarly to establish a new working relationship between the principal and teachers. Communication problems in schools often occur when philosophical differences abound, but are not addressed. A setting in which both teachers and the principal work on a similar goal can provide a chance to reach agreement about what is best for the children and the school. Left unaddressed, differences lead to poor relationships between the principal and teachers, a situation neither party wants.

One extended preK team meeting per month for the remainder of the year followed a similar agenda. The preK teachers and principal gradually became more comfortable with the new way of handling their differences, but there was still work to be done the following year. Due to routine changes in district coaching assignments, I could not continue to lead their meetings.

CHAPTER 17

What do I do now?

The Principal-Consultant Team

SCHOOL LEADERSHIP AT THE BUILDING LEVEL is the most important influence on student learning after researchers account for the quality of classroom instruction. Supporting teachers' professional development is a critical part of a principal's role, yet the reality of the job often leaves too little time for it.[1] The principal discussed in this chapter was no exception. She had no assistant principal to head up instructional leadership in the school or to assign some responsibilities to allow her to do it, and no building-based coaches to support teachers in the classroom. She had some district funding for a school-based professional development (PD) program, but the budget was tight. A few consultants were her key resources. They provided PD sessions for teachers, sometimes did follow-up work in classrooms, and consulted with the principal about teacher development. I (Catherine) became involved with the preK teachers in this school about midyear, after they requested PD to meet their needs. As often happens when a year's PD plan goes awry, this principal was asking, "Okay. What do I do now?" and "How can I prevent this situation in the future?"

As an outside consultant, I provided PD for the preK teachers, follow-up in their classrooms, and assisted the principal in planning PD, schoolwide. The principal allocated time for our meetings late in the day following work in a teacher's classroom; we scheduled other meetings about the group PD series for preK teachers, separately. This principal's willingness to meet had enormous benefits, because without a principal's full support, a consultant's efforts are typically less effective. The principal and I had both been literacy coaches in the district earlier in our careers. Given our common history using a coaching model, we didn't need to set ground rules for our work together this time.

Most of the time, outside coaches (or consultants) and principals cannot assume they will fall into a working relationship easily. Both parties must understand that the purpose of meetings is to inform the principal about the classroom, as the consultant sees it, based on the observation and debriefing with the teacher; or about the content discussed in a group PD session and teachers' reaction to it. In either case, this must be done without suggesting that the consultant's work can substitute for a principal's work with teachers (e.g., supervision, instructional feedback, evaluation). Nor should teachers worry that a consultant is reporting on them in a personal and evaluative way. Thus, ground rules must be established and understood at the start, and a consultant must carefully craft conversations with principals. Meetings with a principal, after a consultant's visit to a classroom or a group PD session for teachers, must be handled with care by both parties.

This principal always asked office staff not to disturb our meetings, short of an emergency, and she stopped ongoing work as soon as I arrived at the agreed-upon time. She set aside fifty minutes for our meetings, took them seriously, and had planned her day's work accordingly. Her journal and pen were on the conference table, ready for note taking. This considerate approach protected her precious time, and mine, too. Other principals sometimes arrived fifteen or twenty minutes past the time set for our meeting, and sometimes left several times to deal with other matters. They also often started our meeting by asking, "What do we need to discuss today?" which indicated that they had not thought about essential agenda items, based on their follow-up work with teachers or some written resources I had provided.

My work in this principal's school had started late in the fall, after the preK teachers requested some afterschool PD sessions focused on emergent writing. They had attended the schoolwide summer institute focused on writing in the elementary school. The principal had hoped that preK and kindergarten teachers could adapt some of the summer institute material, but by late November, the preK team had given up trying. They requested PD focused on their needs. In the first PD session, I offered to observe teachers' writing centers and provide feedback. One teacher invited me. I had already visited once and had met with the principal to discuss the teacher's struggles with classroom management. The principal was less concerned than I, because she thought the situation stemmed more from this teacher's warm and open style than from a lack of management know-how.

I had asked the principal to take another look, if possible, before my next visit to the classroom in two weeks, and to observe briefly in the other teachers' classrooms to see if they also had management issues. If management were a common difficulty, I would adapt one of our three remaining, emergent writing PD sessions to address management issues. After visiting the struggling teacher's classroom for the second time, I headed to the follow-up meeting with the principal.

OUR SECOND MEETING

The principal confirmed that she had the usual fifty minutes for our meeting and said she had read the set of materials on preK writing that I'd also given to the struggling teacher. She had also read the articles about the significance of structure and routines in preK classrooms that I had dropped off more recently. Then, she quickly summarized her thoughts about the follow-up visits to classrooms after our last meeting, indicating that she had concluded that the management of Center Time was not a significant problem across classrooms, and that what she had thought originally were stylistic differences between the struggling teacher and her preK colleagues, she now realized was a lack of management skill.

She said we need not discuss management issues generally today, nor should I modify the afterschool, emergent writing PD sessions. The task now, she said, was figuring out how to support this teacher. She listed her agenda items for today's meeting and asked me to add mine.

- How can I support this teacher in creating an organized yet comfortable environment for her children? Should she visit other classrooms, take a course, continue your visits for a while? Should I make this item part of her evaluation plan?
- How can I improve the hiring process to reduce the need for extensive PD, to avoid time-consuming and expensive help for an individual teacher?
- How can I plan next year's PD to avoid a major midyear modification of the kind needed by preK teachers this year? My goal is to have a yearlong, schoolwide plan, with a central focus for all teachers, but to organize it to meet the needs of all teachers, not just those at one grade level, as happened this year.

OUR DISCUSSION

We agreed that the struggling teacher needed personalized PD for a while, but the principal was concerned that focusing solely on her weakness could make this teacher, new to the staff this year, feel separated from her colleagues. Even though the other teachers were managing Center Time well, the principal thought they probably could still improve their skill, noting that the preK teachers, as a group, often discussed children with challenging behavior in their team meetings. In fact, they had talked in recent meetings about difficult children, especially the one little boy in the struggling teacher's classroom.

Our first thought was that each teacher might select one aspect of classroom management that would improve instruction, not just address a child's challenging behavior. Teachers would get ideas from colleagues, workshops, and readings, and together plan how to solve each teacher's specific problem. I thought a study group, inquiry format might work, but the principal mentioned past problems with that approach:

> We've tried those, and they didn't work. First of all, teachers didn't have time to find readings. When one teacher did find something, the group didn't have time to read the material thoroughly. Everyone tended to skim the readings, and discussions just skimmed the surface of the issue. The second problem, related to the first, was that teachers did not make a specific plan to implement and then assess the outcome. The discussions stayed in the room, never making it into the classroom.

I agreed that study groups must be carefully planned, based on shared interests and needs, and directly applicable to teachers' classrooms.[2] I thought study groups could be effective if they combined what teachers identify as significant classroom-based problems with readings, information from colleagues, and self-reflection. Readings, of course, must be relevant to the specific need. I offered to find readings, including research that would develop teachers' understanding of new practices to try in their classrooms. I stressed encouraging teachers to read more to become better grounded in the research behind effective practices, but acknowledged the difficulty of both finding relevant readings and figuring out specific applications. The principal tentatively agreed to study groups, if I would find the relevant readings, and we moved on to other agenda items.

With regard to the struggling teacher, I reported that, until our meeting today, she had held beliefs that caused her to resist even considering more structure in Center Time. Today, however, she had realized that her current approach to Center Time was getting in the way of goals based on her beliefs. The study group would provide another support for improving her classroom management skills, to supplement the critical, ongoing, individual classroom support. As with most teachers, implementation of new practices is the most difficult part of change, not just realizing that a change is needed. Constructive feedback is essential in the implementation phase.[3] We agreed that I would make two more visits to the struggling teacher's classroom, with debriefs, and then reevaluate. I explained that I'd learned over the years that changing teachers' practices requires a long-term commitment and now expect additions to original PD duties. Principals often think they can prevent these situations by improving hiring practices, as this principal's agenda item indicated, but hiring practices are just the start. There's no such thing as a "natural" teacher, although some personalities and individual circumstances allow quicker progress.

I said that she probably had underestimated the effect of this teacher's prior work context, which included different belief systems and expectations for children's learning, but added that the teacher's work ethic and welcoming attitude toward change and feedback were all positive. I admitted that I had not at first understood why this teacher resisted using more routines to structure Center Time, but that, today, in our meeting, she clearly stated why she didn't want to add more structure, and I realized her resistance was related to philosophy—her belief system. When I provided information that allowed her to realize that her goals for children were in fact undermined by the absence of routines, she was eager to make changes. The points about teacher beliefs struck a chord with the principal: "I sometimes find teachers who claim they want certain outcomes for their students, but just can't seem to bring themselves to implement instruction that supports those outcomes." I indicated the Consortium on Chicago School Research calls the most difficult changes "second order," because these require a shift in beliefs and values, not just practices. First-order changes, however, are more consistent with a teacher's current beliefs and values.[4] That is, first-order changes involve a different way of approaching some aspect of instruction. Once the teacher I worked with today recognized that her practices did not even support her goals for making children more independent and creative, she was willing to put more structure and routines into her classroom.

In the time remaining, we focused more generally on the year's overall PD, with attention to more careful planning for next year and the principal's role in school-based PD. I quickly recapped the current year's PD plan from my outsider's perspective: First, the preK teachers felt the schoolwide PD hadn't met their needs. K teachers have long voiced the same concern. Public schools are only just beginning to adjust to the wider age range now that preK classes are in elementary schools.[5] I added that I am sometimes more concerned about preK and kindergarten teachers accepting that PD designed for older children is appropriate, and trying to apply it to young learners. At least the preK teachers hadn't fallen into that trap.

Second, even though it is important to involve teachers in planning PD, they cannot do it alone. Research suggests that outside consultants enhance the quality of PD.[6] Last year's committee of teachers that planned the summer institute probably thought little about differentiating PD based on the needs of different ages and grade levels. Instead, they just tried to address an issue that was of great concern at some grades, thinking the entire school faculty should know about it and help address it. Much schoolwide PD today focuses on general principles, in this case, effective writing instruction for the elementary grades. Then, the principal relies on periodic teacher team meetings during the year to make adaptations for their age or grade level. However, group PD, including afterschool mini-courses designed to strengthen an area of the curriculum, is not enough.[7] Teachers need additional, classroom-based support and consultation with experts.[8] That's why I offered to visit the classrooms of the preK teachers' attending the afterschool PD sessions on writing.

From my perspective, I said the ideal PD planning process includes these steps:

1. Meet with teachers and visit classrooms briefly to get a sense of what is needed and the context of teachers' work.
2. Meet with the principal to get that perspective.
3. Begin to plan content, check in again, modify as needed.
4. With content confirmed, think about PD pedagogy: How much presentation at first to establish common knowledge of the topic? How much discussion of readings? How much discussion of

ideas and classroom situations? How much collaborative problem solving to include?

5. If possible, check with previous PD providers to learn what pedagogy they used and how it worked. Tailor the PD to the participating teachers' content and instructional needs, and to the principal's view of those needs.

Of course, things often change as I get better acquainted with the participants. Some people think this recursive process is too time consuming and no guarantee for PD success. It is time-consuming, but it gives teachers the same quality of instructional consideration that we ask them to provide to their students, and it makes a consultant's work more effective and often less time consuming, in the long run.

THE PRINCIPAL'S REACTION

The principal nodded in agreement at times, and jotted notes. Then she spoke in a serious tone about her views: "I understand what you are saying, and I wish I had the funding and time to follow that process. In fact, I wish my PD was developed along those lines. I know the impact of quality PD on me, now as a principal and before when I was teaching. But, I just don't see how I can make it happen."

These comments brought us to the role of principal as PD leader. Given this principal's strong work ethic and openness to learning, I said that she could easily become the school's PD leader. Only a few changes would be required in what she was already doing. She should, of course, share responsibility for PD development with teachers. Research has firmly established the value of distributed leadership.[9] At the same time, principals also are the key leaders. If they believe that PD is the leverage point for changing practice and improving outcomes for children, which she did, they must demonstrate their commitment by taking part in selecting the focus of PD, in investigating various options for PD providers, and in participating in group offerings. I stressed that nothing can replace a principal's view of the whole school that comes with the responsible for all the students (and teachers) in it.

The principal stopped taking notes and seemed deep in thought. Before she could question her ability to take on this responsibility, I suggested that, in her case, providing more leadership for PD was not taking on a new role, only changing how she approached it. In short, she needed to oversee and participate in the planning and implementation of PD for her teachers more fully to ensure that these experiences were high quality. Our meeting time was coming to an end and she asked to discuss the principal's role in PD leadership at another time. I said I'd share my copy of *The Principal as Professional Development Leader*, as the basis for our next meeting.[10]

The principal then summarized our discussion. Her summary might serve well as advice to other principals whose schools include preK classrooms, and who agree that PD is about continuously improving a school.

- Effective PD is well planned by the principal and the teachers in consultation with outside expert consultants who may serve as the PD providers.
- PD is differentiated for teachers, according to the levels they teach and their previous experiences and expertise, and is modified as needed in response to participants' needs.
- Group PD sessions are only one component of effective professional development. Improvements in instruction are more likely when in-class coaching is provided to teachers by someone with more expertise than the group PD provider.
- PD plans that meet the needs of the whole school are long term and continuously evolving.
- The principal and consultant must work as a team. The principal has knowledge of the whole school and specific responsibilities for supervising teachers, providing instructional feedback, and evaluation. The consultant or coach brings deep knowledge of the content, instructional practices, and characteristics

of learning found at specific ages and grade levels. A consultant supports individual teachers to change their practices.

Many principals often view PD as an add-on, in response to problems as they emerge. A more realistic view is that PD is a lifeline for school improvement. Through careful planning that follows guidelines established by research, PD can provide teachers with continuous professional learning.[11]

CHAPTER 18

I don't want to just house preK classrooms in my building.

A Model Principal's View of PreK

ALTHOUGH MOST PRINCIPALS take seriously the responsibility of having preK classrooms in their buildings, some underestimate both the importance of educating four-year-olds and the complexity involved. This chapter is about one principal who did *not* underestimate the importance or the complexity of educating preschool-age children, and my experience working in his school, just as it added two preK classrooms.

I (Catherine) met John after giving a presentation on the topic of full-day kindergarten programs to the principals in a small urban district. After the presentation, he asked me to give a presentation on the same topic for his K–5 school faculty at their next schoolwide PD meeting. I had never been asked to speak to an entire elementary school faculty about kindergarten, and I asked what he hoped to accomplish for the kindergarten teachers in his building:

Oh, I'm not doing this for the kindergarten teachers, but to help our two new preK classes become more fully integrated into the school. Many people who have children think that working with four- and five-year-olds comes easily, and is mostly about having fun. Your remarks today reminded me that early childhood teachers must study children and craft learning experiences carefully. I don't want to just house preK classrooms in my building. In my school, I want the preK experience to be viewed as children's official entry into education, the important first step to their school achievement. To make that a reality, I need all teachers in the building to understand the value of early learning and teaching.

SOME BACKGROUND

The assistant superintendent in John's district had invited me to deliver the keynote at an all-day PD session for the district's kindergarten teachers, when they were moving from half-day to full-day sessions, because many teachers had reservations about this change. My task was to ease their concerns by relating my experience with schools that had already gone through this transition. I focused on the thinking behind a move to full-day kindergarten, especially on the opportunity for more center-based learning, now that academic skills instruction consumed considerable time in a half-day program.

The teachers agreed about the opportunities that a full-day kindergarten provided, but worried their principals might not see it in this way. After hearing these concerns, the assistant superintendent asked me to repeat my presentation to the principals of the district's eight elementary schools and to lead a discussion about the benefits of full-day kindergarten afterward. John, one of the principals in attendance, had been a principal of one of the K–5 schools in the district for several years. Before that, he was a classroom teacher in several different grades and then an assistant principal in another building in the district.

As we talked, John explained that he worked hard as a principal to maintain a positive school climate and encouraged teacher collaboration. He thought teachers enjoyed working in his building, in part because of his approach to problems and careful attention to seemingly ordinary issues. He said that none of the faculty had been surprised to hear that their school was also an option for a new preK classroom, or that he had requested two classrooms, not just one, out of concern that just one teacher at any grade level might feel isolated. After hiring the new preK teachers, John had invited them to the school to see their classrooms, meet faculty colleagues, and become familiar with school resources. He welcomed them to come in over the summer before starting in the fall and gave them his cellphone number, should they have questions.

When school began in the fall, John watched closely to see how the preK teachers worked together and also whether they turned to any other teachers for support and advice. By November, they had become part of the school's social fabric, but not as much a part of the professional structure of the school as he would have liked. For example, they were quiet at faculty meetings and often shared a concern at meetings with the principal that the elementary teachers did not see their work as real teaching. John also had overheard comments about how lucky the preK teachers were, with no worries about grade-level benchmarks (i.e., formal testing) for academic learning. Of course, preK teachers must attend to early learning standards, and meet expectations stipulated in them. These comments were not malicious, but did have the effect of setting the preK teachers apart from the rest of the faculty, professionally. John knew their contribution was vital to children's later academic success and thought I could convince the whole faculty of the importance of preK in laying the foundation for a child's later achievement. I thought I could at least get the conversation started. John also asked for help in planning follow-up to this initial PD, to strengthen the view in his school that theirs was a "preK–5 place of learning." Though my relationship with the school would be short term, John considered us partners. The possibility of working with the faculty in a school with this kind of leader appealed to me, and we began.

BEGINNING THE WORK

I requested a school walk-through with John before starting to plan my talk so I could make it more relevant to this school. We set a date that wouldn't disrupt teachers' plans, and John let all teachers know that the purpose of the visit was to give me a sense of the school and some context for the PD session. As we visited classrooms, teachers and children greeted John warmly and shared their work. When time permitted, we sat down and talked with children. Classrooms across the grades were busy with lots of chatter, yet very focused. The interactions between teachers and children were positive and productive, and John and the teachers interacted comfortably. The tone for the school was friendly and learning-oriented. During the walk-through, John explained curricula, district priorities for the year, and his perceptions of teachers' struggles.

Back in his office, I commented about the school climate and asked how it had come about. John said he mostly modeled the behaviors he wanted to see from others. Over time, teachers and parents understood that he meant what he said and walked his talk. It was John's attention to school climate that made him particularly observant of teacher-child and teacher-teacher interactions, which is how he had picked up on the superficial integration of the preK teachers in the school's professional life. When I expressed concern that teachers in grades one through five might not see the relevance of my presentation to their work, he said, "They're accustomed to my attempts to broaden their horizons. I often bring in new topics for us to investigate and consider in terms of how we might improve teaching and learning." It was comforting to know this faculty was accustomed to experiences intended to broaden their thinking, but I still wanted John's input about how to shape my PowerPoint slides for this audience.

As we reviewed the original slides from the principals' meeting, John indicated ones that were probably irrelevant, others that teachers probably needed to see, and still others they needed to both see and discuss. In the past, I had often wanted good feedback when preparing a presentation for teachers, but rarely got it. A principal would say, "Oh, any information you can provide will be a great help," or, "You're the expert. Do what you think will work best for our teachers." Knowing their audience before meeting them helps PD providers sort out which points to emphasize and the difficulties teachers might raise. Both the walk-through and the planning conversation provided background about this school that helped me tailor the talk, and I began to finalize the presentation's key points.

Final Preparation

I now knew the climate in this school, John's support for teacher collaboration, and his vision of a school as a "preK–fifth-grade place of learning." An entire afternoon was set aside for the PD session, which allowed time for some interaction. I first inserted a few questions to prompt teachers to share their views with one another in a small group and then report a summary of their group's main points to everyone. I also wanted some time for a working session in which a group of teachers from across the range of classrooms would trace the development of a fifth-grade benchmark, all the way from preK. I wanted, in this case, both to get the teachers to think about the school as a whole and to set the stage for future work sessions, where I knew from John that teachers would be asked to think beyond their own grade levels.

I double-checked plans with John as they emerged and asked that he review the whole presentation to make sure the afternoon would be productive for the teachers. John also provided teachers with information, an "advance warning," he called it, about what the session would entail. He included a brief overview of the topics included and a bit of background about my experiences. He also introduced me nicely on the day of the PD, using his personal experience in the previous session for principals, but moving on from there to the school mission:

> After hearing Catherine speak about the transition from half-day to full-day kindergarten, and about the significance of high-quality preschools in preparing children for today's kindergartens, I thought I'd try to take advantage of her for our school. We're now able to follow children from preschool to middle school, and we'll learn as we go and adjust instruction for all our children. Today marks the

beginning of my renewed interest in providing children with truly seamless curriculum and instruction. I look forward to continuing our work together.

These remarks made it clear that preK was not an add-on in this school, but an integral component that helped make the school's mission possible.

THE AFTERNOON SESSION

In the PD session, the teachers were interested in the information about the relationship between preK and kindergarten and other grades, and eager to ask questions and comment. There were three main topics for the day:

- Today's kindergartens differ from those of twenty years ago, not just because of the current focus on academics. They differ because we have learned so much in recent years about young children's learning. Literacy is a case in point, and I provided examples.[1]
- Research on preschoolers has led to an increase in preK programs, as well as serious discussions about their quality.[2] It has also highlighted the value of engaging young children in authentic learning experiences and the significance of intentional teaching.[3]
- Current high expectations for achievement in the elementary school require us to build a strong foundation in both skills and knowledge from early on.[4] No longer can we wait until first grade, or beyond, to begin.

The small-group discussions were lively and, as always, revealed personal beliefs. When grade-level groups of teachers were asked to delineate "appropriate expected outcomes of preK" and how they aligned with their grade level, group responses and conversations were varied and somewhat as I had expected, though not entirely. Interestingly, kindergarten teachers emphasized early literacy skills, whereas upper-grade teachers focused more on self-regulatory behavior and habits of mind—willingness to problem solve and persist in projects, to think somewhat flexibly, to consider classmates' thinking. This was intriguing, because in my experience, teachers often seem to feel that the previous grade should focus primarily on what children will face in the next, and little on what comes two or three grades beyond that.

With regard to preK and kindergarten, however, research indicates clearly that two strands of learning must be launched, one focusing on literacy and numeracy skills, the other on oral language, content knowledge, and higher-level thinking.[5] The skills are needed for learning to read and to begin formal instruction in mathematics, but oral language, content knowledge, and higher-level thinking must also start early, because it takes years to build language and concepts that form the foundation for schoolwork in the fourth and fifth grades. And habits of mind are just that. Preschoolers, even babies, learn how to interact with the world, how to think about literacy skills and number, and everything else. PreK and kindergarten teachers rarely get to hear what fourth- and fifth-grade teachers hope children learn in the early childhood years. What's interesting is that some of what fourth- and fifth-grade teachers want is consistent with traditional preK education that was at one time more cognitive than academic and included experiences that supported the social skills that matter for learning (e.g., attending to tasks, persisting in the face of challenges, collaborating positively with peers).[6]

Throughout the whole-group discussion, K–5 teachers kept warning preK teachers that they were expected to fully prepare the whole child for the formal instruction they would experience in the grades. Little was said about changing the grades to better match the way young children learn, but that probably would emerge in future meetings. It might not have been as big an issue in this school, anyway, given the active and collaborative learning I had observed during the walk-through visit.

Working in vertical teams, teachers chose one of the literacy or math benchmark skills and traced its development from preK to fifth grade. This task required analysis of what was involved in the benchmark, delineation of where the prerequisite skills were learned in other grades, and how it got started in preK. Because the teachers were accustomed to collaborating, they didn't hesitate to ask colleagues on other teams for help, and teachers sometimes went to their classrooms to get resources to bring to the meeting room.

Teachers found it difficult to trace the trajectory of fifth-grade benchmark skills from preK, but they persevered and indicated an interest in getting better at this. One teacher commented that figuring out how every grade contributed to a child's achievement was going to make each teacher more reliant on all the other teachers in the school. She said that although all teachers did occasionally talk with one another, they tended to rely mostly on grade-level colleagues and to worry about grade-level issues, and often "lost sight of the big picture." Another teacher commented about how hard it was to do a trajectory, and that everyone needed to get out their books and study up, "because we don't always really even know enough about our own grade levels." She added that perhaps I knew where to find trajectories already mapped out! I explained that prepared trajectories are only helpful after you have spent some time trying to develop them: "It's rather like those number line strips that kindergarten teachers sometimes give to children. Children can use those productively only after they have developed a conceptual number line through concrete experiences with number."

NEXT STEPS

John was an active participant throughout the PD session. He joined different groups at various times and added to the discussion or task at hand, even volunteering to chart the trajectory in one group, as teachers generated items. Immediately following the meeting, we discussed the very positive outcome of the session. He felt that the teachers left with more appreciation for the potential outcomes of high-quality preK. I was pleased with the teachers' receptivity to digging deeply into areas about which they had little knowledge and no experience. We agreed that, at least for now, teachers felt a shared responsibility for children's success and a willingness to work together toward that end.

Realistically, we knew that these outcomes could be short-lived without ongoing, yearlong work. We agreed to meet the following week to plan what to do next to maintain the group's focus and momentum. At that meeting, we agreed to some tasks for John:

- He would ask for input from the preK teachers at faculty meetings if they did not offer it spontaneously. Because he did not want the preK teachers to feel they had been put on the spot, he would preface questions or requests with a comment that linked the discussion point to preK (e.g., "How do you handle . . . in preK?" "Are there strategies you use that might be helpful here?").
- Periodically, time in group meetings would be devoted to continuing the trajectory work. John thought doing more work of this kind would help the teachers develop a deeper understanding of teaching and learning. It would also prompt teacher discussion in vertical teams that led to thinking beyond each teacher's grade level.
- Later in the year, John would ask the preK teachers to share a snapshot of their day, using a slide show or video at a schoolwide teacher meeting. He would remind them to come prepared to explain why they structured the schedule, organized the classroom, and implemented lessons as they did. He knew they had already done something similar for Parents Night, and felt a version for a teachers' meeting would not require starting from scratch.
- Last, John would make connections to the preK (and other grades) when he spoke with individual teachers or grade-level teams. Again, the goal was to model the kind of thinking in which he hoped the teachers would engage. As an example, he said he might say to a first-grade teacher who was worried about teaching persuasive writing to "remember that the children had done some persuasive talking in both kindergarten and preK, and had observed and probably discussed how characters in stories

had persuaded other characters." John had the same goals for himself as he held for the teachers in the building.

FOLLOW-UP

My relationship with John's school ended with that meeting due to outside events, but I occasionally heard from other personnel in the district that John focused the rest of the year on making preK an integral part of his school. Across the district, he continued to advocate strongly for preK as the first phase of a child's schooling and spoke highly about the contributions preK teachers make to an elementary school. He probably encountered hurdles along the way, but this principal could show others what it meant to be a strong leader for early childhood education.

As a school leader, John first set the tone for the school. With a positive school climate as a backdrop, he then made clear his irrefutable support of preK. Furthermore, he demonstrated this regard in his interactions throughout each day. Equally important, John knew how to support a consultant for the benefit of his faculty. He invited me to support his effort, but unlike most other principals, he partnered with me in a very substantial way. He shared his views of the school and what his teachers needed, and he attended closely to the details of the PD session. His attention to my planning was central to the session's success.

John also partnered with the teachers. Throughout that first PD session, he participated actively by adding to the conversation, working on tasks, and sometimes thinking out loud. He conveyed through his actions a commitment to preK–5 teaching and learning and a willingness to work hard to make it work. John truly understood the importance of the principal as an instructional leader. He was on the ground in classrooms, attended all PD sessions, listened and read, shared his thoughts, and thought of himself as a learner, alongside everyone else. In other words, he modeled the kind of thinking and collaborating he advocated—he led by example.

NOTES

Chapter 1

1. Lee S. Shulman, "Those Who Understand: Knowledge Growth in Teaching," *Educational Researcher* 15, no. 2 (1985): 4–14.
2. Anne McGill-Franzen, "In the Press to Scale Up, What Is at Risk?," *Reading Research Quarterly* 40, no. 3 (2005): 366–70; Sheila W. Valencia, Nancy A. Place, Susan D. Martin, and Pamela Grossman, "Curriculum Materials for Elementary Reading: Shackles and Scaffolds for Four Beginning Teachers," *The Elementary School Journal* 107, no.1 (2009): 93–120.
3. John E. Anderson, "Child Development: An Historical Perspective," *Child Development* 27, no. 2 (1956): 181–96.
4. Ibid.
5. William Teale," Young Children and Reading: Trends Across the Twentieth Century," *The Journal of Education* 177, no. 3 (1995): 95–127.
6. James Hymes, *Before the Child Reads* (White Plains, NY: Row, Peterson and Company, 1958) 12–13.
7. Ibid., 22–23; 25.
8. Joe McVicker Hunt, *Intelligence and Experience* (New York: The Ronald Press, 1961), 363.
9. Mary C. Day and Ronald K. Parker, *The Preschool in Action: Exploring Early Childhood Programs* (Boston: Allyn & Bacon, 1977).
10. Sue Bredekamp, ed., *Developmentally Appropriate Practice in Early Childhood Programs Serving Children from Birth through Age 8* (Washington, DC: NAEYC, 1987); Sue Bredekamp and Carol Copple, eds., *Developmentally Appropriate Practice in Early Childhood Programs*, rev. ed. (Washington, DC: NAEYC, 1997); Susan B. Neuman, Carol Copple, and Sue Bredekamp, *Learning to Read and Write: Developmentally Appropriate Practices for Young Children* (Washington, DC: NAEYC, 2000); Carol Copple and Sue

Bredekamp, eds., *Developmentally Appropriate Practice in Early Childhood Programs Serving Children from Birth through Age 8*, 3rd ed. (Washington, DC: NAEYC, 2009).

11. Marilyn J. Adams, *Beginning to Read* (Cambridge, MA: The MIT Press, 1990); Catherine Snow, M. Susan Burns, and Peg Griffin, eds., *Preventing Reading Difficulties in Young Children* (Washington, DC: National Academy Press, 1998).

12. William H. Teale and Elizabeth Sulzby, *Emergent Literacy: Writing and Reading* (Norwood, NJ: Ablex Publishing Corporation, 1986).

13. Jessica L. Hoffman, "Looking Back and Looking Forward: Lessons Learned from Early Reading First," *Childhood Education* 87, no. 3 (2010).

14. Carole Greenes, Herbert P. Ginsburg, and Robert Balfanz, "Big Math for Little Kids," *Early Childhood Research Quarterly* 19, no. 1 (2004): 159–66; Julie Sarama and Douglas H. Clements, "Building Blocks for Early Childhood Mathematics," *Early Childhood Research Quarterly* 19, no. 1 (2004): 181–89.

15. W. Steven Barnett, *Getting the Facts Right on Pre-K and the President's Pre-K Proposal* (New Brunswick, NJ: NIEER, 2013); W. Steven Barnett, Effectiveness of Early Educational Interventions, *Science* 333, no. 6045 (2001): 975–78; W. Steven Barnett and Donald J. Yarosz, "Who Goes to Preschool and Why Does It Matter," *NIEER Preschool Policy Brief* 15, no. 15 (2006).

16. Katherine B. Stevens and Elizabeth English, *Does PreK Work? The Research on Ten Early Childhood Programs—and What It Tells Us* (Washington, DC: The American Enterprise Institute for Public Policy Research, 2016): 1.

17. Mark W. Lipsey, Dale C. Farran, and Kerry G. Hofer, *A Randomized Trial of a Statewide Voluntary Prekindergarten Program on Children's Skills and Behaviors through Third Grade*, research report (Nashville, TN: Vanderbilt University, Peabody Research Institute, 2015).

18. Dale C. Farran, "We Need More Evidence in Order to Create Effective Pre-K Programs," *Economic Studies at Brookings, Evidence Speaks Reports* 1, no. 11 (February 2016): 1–6.

19. Ibid., 3–5; Robert C. Pianta, Karen M. LaParo, and Bridget K. Hamre, *Classroom Assessment Scoring System Manual PreK* (Baltimore, MD: Paul H. Brookes, 2008); Thelma Harms, Richard M. Clifford, and Debbie Cryer, *The Early Childhood Environments Rating Scale—Revised* (New York:

Teachers College Press, 2005); W. Steven Barnett, Megan E. Carolan, James H. Squires, Kirsty Clarke Brown, et al., *The State of Preschool 2014* (New Brunswick, NJ: National Institute for Early Childhood Research, 2015), 24.

20. Dale C. Farran, "Federal Preschool Development Grants: Evaluation Needed," *Economic Studies at Brookings, Evidence Speaks Reports* 1, no. 22 (July 14, 2016) 1–6.

21. Robert D. Putnam, *Our Kids: The American Dream in Crisis* (New York: Simon & Schuster, 2015); Sean F. Reardon, "The Widening Academic Achievement Gap between the Rich and Poor: New Evidence and Possible Explanation," in *Whither Opportunity?: Rising Inequality, Schools, and Children's Life Choice*, eds. Greg J. Duncan and Richard J. Murnane (New York: Russell Sage and Spencer Foundation, 2011), 91–115; Sean F. Reardon, "The Widening Income Gap," *Educational Leadership* 70, no. 8 (2013): 10–16.

22. Anitha Mohan and Christina Walker, *Head Start Participants, Programs, Families, and Staff in 2014* (Washington, DC: Center for Law and Social Policy, 2016); Putnam, *Our Kids*; Reardon, "The Widening Academic Achievement Gap."

23. Steven S. Barnett, Kristy Brown, and Rima Shore, "The Universal vs. Targeted Debate: Should the United States Have Preschool for All?," *Preschool Policy Matters*, no. 6 (New Brunswick, NJ: National Institute for Early Education Research, 2004); Jeanne L. Reid and Sharon L Kagan, *A Better Start: Why Classroom Diversity Matters in Early Education* (New York: The Century Foundation; Washington, DC: Poverty & Race Research Action Council, 2013).

Part I

1. Carol Copple and Sue Bredekamp, eds., *Developmentally Appropriate Practice in Early Childhood Programs*, 3rd ed. (Washington, DC: NAEYC, 2009); Susan B. Neuman, Carol Copple, and Sue Bredekamp, eds., *Learning to Read and Write: Developmentally Appropriate Practices for Young Children* (Washington, DC: NAEYC, 2000); Thelma Harms, Richard M. Clifford, and Debbie Cryer, *The Early Childhood Rating Scale-Revised* (New York: Teachers College Press, 2005); C. Cybele Raver, Christine ·

Li-Grining, Kristen Bub, Stephanie Jones et al., "CSRP's Impact on Low-Income Preschoolers' Preacademic Skills: Self-Regulation as a Mediating Mechanism," *Child Development* 82, no. 1 (2011): 362–78.

2. Timothy Shanahan, "Thinking with the Research: Research Changes Its Mind (Again)," *The Reading Teacher* 70, no. 1 (2016): 245–48; William H. Teale, Jessica L. Hoffman, and Kathleen Paciga, "Where Is NELP Leading Preschool Literacy Instruction? Potential Positives and Pitfalls," *Educational Researcher* 39, no. 4 (2010): 311–15.

3. Richard Allington and P. David Pearson, "The Casualties of Policy on Early Literacy Development," *Language Arts* 89, no. 1 (2011): 70–74; Anne McGill-Franzen, "In the Press to Scale Up, What Is at Risk?," *Reading Research Quarterly* 40, no. 3 (2005): 366–70; Sheila W. Valencia, Susan D. Martin, Nancy A. Place, and Pam L. Grossman, "Complex Interactions in Student Teaching: Lost Opportunities for Learning," *Journal of Teacher Education* 60, no. 3 (2009): 304–22.

4. Laura M. Justice, Andrew J. Mashburn, Bridget K. Hamre, and Robert C. Pianta, "Quality of Language and Literacy Instruction in Preschool Classrooms Serving At-Risk Pupils," *Early Childhood Research Quarterly* 23, no.1 (2008): 51–68; Andrew J. Mashburn, Robert C. Pianta, Oscar Barbarin, and Donna Bryant et al., "Measures of Classroom Quality in Prekindergarten and Children's Development of Academic, Language, and Social Skills," *Child Development* 79, no. 3 (2008): 732–49.

Chapter 2

1. Ezra Jack Keats, *The Snowy Day* (New York: Viking Press, 1962).

2. Sonia Q. Cabell, Laura M. Justice, Carol Vukelich, Martha Jane Buell, and Myae Han, "Strategic and Intentional Shared Storybook Reading," in *Achieving Excellence in Preschool Literacy Instruction*, eds., Laura M. Justice and Carol Vukelich (New York: Guilford Press, 2008), 198–220; Anita S McGinty, Amy Sofka, Margaret Sutton, and Laura Justice, "Fostering Print Awareness through Interactive Shared Reading," in *Sharing Books and Stories to Promote Language and Literacy*, ed., Anne van Kleeck (San Diego: Plural Publishing, 2009), 77–117; Helen K. Ezell and Laura M. Justice, *Shared Storybook Reading* (Baltimore, MD: Paul H. Brookes, 2005), 87–117.

3. Anne van Kleeck, "Fostering Letter Knowledge in Prereaders During Book Sharing: New Perspectives and Cultural Issues," in van Kleeck, *Sharing Books and Stories*, 121–46.

4. Jeanne R. Paratore, Christina M. Cassano, and Judith A. Schickedanz, "Supporting Early (and Later) Literacy Development at Home and at School: The Long View," in *Handbook of Reading Research*, vol. IV, eds., Michael L. Kamil, P. David Pearson, Elizabeth Birr Moje, and Peter P. Afflerbach (New York: Routledge, 2011), 107–35.

5. McGinty et al., "Fostering Print Awareness," 90–93.

6. Cabell et al., "Strategic and Intentional Shared Book Reading," 203–204.

Chapter 3

1. Anne Hass Dyson, "Symbol Makers, Symbol Weavers: How Children Link Play, Pictures, and Print," *Young Children* 45, no. 2 (1990): 50–57.

2. Claire E. Cameron and Frederick J. Morrison, "Teacher Activity Orienting Predicts Preschoolers' Academic and Self-Regulatory Skills," *Early Education & Development* 22, no. 4 (2011): 620–48.

3. Lori Norton-Meier and Kathryn F. Whitmore, "Developmental Moments: Teacher Decision-Making to Support Young Writers," *Young Children* 70, no. 4 (2015): 76–83; Judith A. Schickedanz and Molly F. Collins, *So Much More Than the ABCs* (Washington, DC: NAEYC, 2013), see chapters 6 and 8.

4. Leo Lionni, *It's Mine* (New York: Scholastic, Inc., 1985).

5. Nancy Ratcliff, "Use the Environment to Prevent Discipline Problems and Support Learning," *Young Children* 56, no. 5 (2001): 84–88.

6. Cameron and Morrison, "Teacher Activity Orienting Predicts Preschoolers' Academic and Self-Regulatory Skills."

7. Amanda P. Williford, Michelle F. Maier, Jason T. Downer, Robert C. Pianta, and Carollee Howes, "Understanding How Children's Engagement and Teachers' Interactions Combine to Predict School Readiness," *Journal of Applied Developmental Psychology* 34, no. 6 (2013): 299–309.

8. Ibid.

9. Sara E. Rimm-Kaufman, Tim W. Curby, Kevin J. Grimm, Lori Nathanson, and Laura L. Brock. "The Contribution of Children's Self-Regulation and

Classroom Quality to Children's Adaptive Behaviors in the Kindergarten Classroom," *Developmental Psychology* 45, no.4 (2009): 958–72.

10. Mary Wagner Fuhs, Dale C. Farran, and Kimberly Turner Nesbitt, "Preschool Classroom Processes as Predictors of Children's Cognitive Self-Regulation Skills Development," *School Psychology Quarterly* 28, no. 4 (2013): 347–59.

Chapter 4

1. NAEYC, "10 Ways to Use the Sensory Table," *Teaching Young Children* 8, no. 1 (2014): 6–7; Cindy Hoisington, Ingrid Chalufour, Jeff Winokur, and Nancy Clark-Chiarelli, "Promoting Children's Science Inquiry and Learning through Water Investigations," *Young Children* 69, no. 4 (2014): 74–79.

2. Robert C. Pianta, Karen M. LaParo, and Bridget K. Hamre, *Classroom Assessment Scoring System, PreK Manual* (Baltimore, MD: Paul H. Brookes, 2008), 43–54.

Chapter 5

1. Katherine Nelson, *Young Minds in Social Worlds: Experience, Meaning, and Memory* (Cambridge, MA: Harvard University Press, 2007), 209.

2. Betty Hart and Todd T. Risley, *The Social World of Children Learning to Talk* (Baltimore, MD: Paul H. Brookes, 1999).

3. Sara E. Rimm-Kaufman, Tim W. Curby, Kevin J. Grimm, Lori Nathanson, and Laura L. Brock, "The Contribution of Children's Self-Regulation and Classroom Quality to Children's Adaptive Behaviors in the Kindergarten Classroom," *Developmental Psychology* 45 no. 4 (2009): 958–72.

4. C. Cybele Raver, Stephanie M. Jones, Christine Li-Grining, and Fuhua Zhai et al., "CSRP's Impact on Low-Income Preschoolers' Preacademic Skills: Self-Regulation as a Mediating Mechanism," *Child Development* 82, no. 1 (2011): 362–78.

5. Claire E. Cameron and Frederick J. Morrison, "Teacher Activity Orienting Predicts Preschoolers' Academic and Self-Regulatory Skills," *Early Education & Development* 22, no. 4 (2011): 620–48.

6. Sheila W. Valencia, Nancy A. Price, Susan D. Martin, and Pamela Grossman, "Curriculum Materials for Elementary Reading: Shackles and

Scaffold for Four Beginning Teachers," *Elementary School Journal* 107, no. 1 (2006): 93–120.

7. Anne McGill-Franzen, "In the Press to Scale Up, what Is at Risk?," *Reading Research Quarterly* 40, no. 3 (2005): 366–70.

Part II

1. James L. Hymes, *Before the Child Reads* (White Plains, NY: Row, Peterson and Company, 1958), 20–25.

2. Leslie B. Cohen and Barbara A. Younger, "Infant Perception of Angular Relations," *Infant Behavior and Development* 7, no. 1 (1984): 37–47; Peter J. Eimas and Paul Quinn, "Studies of the Formation of Perceptually-Based Basic Level Categories in Young Infants," *Child Development* 65, no. 3 (1994): 903–17.

3. Isabelle Y. Liberman, Donald Shankweiler, F. William Fischer, and Bonnie Carter, "Explicit Syllable and Phoneme Segmentation," *Journal of Experimental Child Psychology* 18, no. 2 (1974): 201–12.

4. Daphne Bassok, Scott Latham, and Anna Rorem, "Is Kindergarten the New First Grade?," *AERA Open* 1, no. 4 (2016): 1–31.

5. Carol Copple and Sue Bredekamp, eds., *Developmentally Appropriate Practice in Early Childhood Programs*, 3rd ed. (Washington, DC: NAEYC, 2009), 11.

6. Kenneth Ginsburg and the Committee on Communications and Committee on Psychosocial Aspects of Child and Family Health, "The Importance of Play in Promoting Healthy Child Development and Maintaining Strong Parent-Child Bonds," *Pediatrics* 119, no. 1 (2007):182–91.

7. Greg J. Duncan, Chantelle J. Dowsett, Amy Claessens, and Katherine Magnuson et al., "School Readiness and Later Achievement," *Developmental Psychology* 43, no. 6 (2007): 1428–46; Megan M. McClelland, Claire E. Cameron, Carol M. Connor, and Carrie L. Farris et al., "Links between Behavioral Regulation and Preschoolers' Literacy, Vocabulary, and Math Skills," *Developmental Psychology* 43, no. 4 (2007): 947–59; Clancy Blair, "Integrating Cognition and Emotion in Neurobiological Conceptualization of Children's Functioning at School Entry," *American Psychologist* 57, no. 2 (2002):111–27; 1 Carlos Valiente, Jodi Swanson, and Nancy Eisenberg, "Linking Students' Emotions and

Academic Achievement: When and Why Emotions Matter," *Child Development Perspectives* 6, no. 2 (2012): 129–35.

8. Dale C. Farran and Mark W. Lipsey, "Expectations of Sustained Effects from Scaled Up Pre-K: Challenges from the Tennessee Study," *Evidence Speaks Reports* 1, no. 4 (Washington, DC: Brookings, 2015), 1–7.

9. Ibid.

Chapter 6

1. Billie Enz and James F. Christie, "Teacher Play Interaction Styles and Their Impact on Children's Oral Language and Literacy Play" (paper presented at the 43rd annual meeting of the National Reading Conference, Charleston, SC, 1993).

2. Sohyun Meacham, Carol Vukelich, Myae Han, and Martha Buell, "Teachers' Responsiveness to Preschoolers' Utterances in Sociodramatic Play," *Early Education and Development* 27, no. 3 (2016): 318–35.

3. Deena Skolnick Weisberg, Jennifer M. Zosh, Kathy Hirsh-Pasek, and Roberta Michnick Golinkoff, "Talking It Up: Play, Language development, and the Role of Adult Support," *American Journal of Play* 6, no. 1 (2013): 39–54.

4. Angeline S. Lillard, Matthew D. Lerner, Emily J. Hopkins, Rebecca A. Dore, Eric D. Smith, and Carolyn M. Palmquist, "The Impact of Pretend Play on Children's Development: A Review of the Evidence," *Psychological Bulletin* 139, no. 1 (2013): 1–34; Anthony D. Pellegrini and Lee Galda, "Ten Years Later: A Reexamination of Symbolic Play and Literacy Research," *Reading Research Quarterly* 28, no. 20 (1993): 162–75; Susan B. Neuman and Kathleen Roskos, "Literacy Knowledge in Practice: Contexts of Participation for Young Writers and Readers," *Reading Research Quarterly* 32, no. 4 (1997): 10–32.

5. Kathleen Coolahan, John Fantuzzo, Julia Mendez, and Paul McDermott, "Preschool Peer Interactions and Readiness to Learn: Relationships between Classroom Peer Play and Learning Behaviors and Conduct," *Journal of Educational Psychology* 92, no. 3 (2000): 458–65.

6. John Fantuzzo, Brian Sutton-Smith, Marc Atkins, Raymond Meyers, Howard Stevenson, Kathleen Coolahan, Andrea Weiss, and Patricia Manz, "Community-Based Resilient Peer Treatment of Withdrawn

Maltreated Preschool Children," *Journal of Consulting and Clinical Psychology* 64, no. 6 (1996): 1377–86.

7. Dale C. Farran and Mark W. Lipsey, "Expectations of Sustained Effects from Scaled Up PreK: Challenges from the Tennessee Study," *Economic Studies at Brookings*, *Evidence Speaks Reports* 1, no. 3 (2015): 1–7.

Chapter 7

1. Amy Claessens and Mimi Engel, "How Important Is Where You Start? Early Mathematics Knowledge and Later School Success," *Teachers College Record* 115, no. 66 (2013): 1–29; David. J. Purpura, Arthur J. Baroody, and Christopher J. Lonigan, "The Transition from Informal to Formal Mathematical Knowledge: Mediation by Numerical Knowledge," *Journal of Educational Psychology* 105, no. 2 (2013): 453–64.

2. Greg J. Duncan, Chantelle J. Dowsett, Amy Claessens, and Katherine Magnuson et al., "School Readiness and Later Achievement," *Developmental Psychology* 43, no. 6 (2007): 1428–46; Christopher J. Lonigan, Beth M. Phillips, Jeanine L. Clancy, and Susan H. Landry et al., "Impacts of a Comprehensive School Readiness Curriculum for Preschool Children at Risk for Educational Difficulties," *Child Development* 86, no. 6 (2015): 1773–93.

3. Deena Skolnick Weisberg, Kathy Hirsh-Pasek, and Roberta Michnick Golinkoff, "Guided Play: Where Curricular Goals Meet a Playful Pedagogy," *Mind, Brain, and Education* 7, no. 2 (2013):104–12.

4. Candice M. Mills, Judith H. Danovitch, Meredith G. Grant, and Fadwa B. Elashi, "Little Pitchers Use Their Big Ears: Preschoolers Solve Problems by Listening to Others Ask Questions," *Child Development* 83, no. 2 (2012): 568–80.

5. Douglas H. Clements, "Subitizing: What Is It? Why Teach It?," *Teaching Children Mathematics* 5, no. 7 (1999): 400–405.

6. Phyllis Root and Jane Chapman, illustrator, *One Duck Stuck* (Cambridge, MA: Candlewick Press, 1998); Eric Carle, *The Very Hungry Caterpillar* (New York: Philomel Books, 1987).

7. Eve Merriam and Bernie Karlin, illustrator, *12 Ways to Get to 11* (New York: Simon & Schuster Books for Young Readers, 1993).

8. Kevin Crowley, Maureen A. Callanan, Jennifer L. Jipson, and Jodi Galco

et al., "Shared Scientific Thinking in Everyday Parent-Child Activity,"
Science Education 85, no.6 (2001): 712–32.

Chapter 8

1. Lea M. McGee and Donald J. Richgels, "K is Kristen's," *The Reading
   Teacher* 39, no. 2 (1989): 216–25; Rebecca Trieman and Victor Broderick,
   "What's in a Name: Children's Knowledge about the Letters in Their
   Own Names," *Journal of Experimental Child Psychology* 70, no. 1(1998):
   97–116; Jodi G. Welsh, Amie Sullivan, and Laura M. Justice, "That's My
   Letter!: What Preschoolers' Name Writing Representations Tell about
   Emergent Literacy Knowledge," *Journal of Literacy Research* 35, no. 2
   (2003):757–76.
2. National Early Literacy Panel Report (NELP), *Developing Early Literacy:
   Report of the National Early Literacy Panel* (Washington, DC: National
   Institute for Literacy, 2008).
3. William H. Teale, Jessica L. Hoffman, and Kathleen A Paciga, "Where is
   NELP Leading Preschool Literacy Instruction? Potential Positives and
   Pitfalls," *Educational Researcher* 39, no. 4 (2010): 311–15.
4. National Early Literacy Panel Report, *Developing Early Literacy*.
5. Michelle Drouin and Jenna Harmon, "Name Writing and Letter
   Knowledge in Preschoolers: Incongruities in Skills and the Usefulness of
   Name Writing as a Developmental Indicator," *Early Childhood Research
   Quarterly* 24, no. 3 (2009): 263–70; Karen E. Diamond, Hope K. Gerde,
   and Douglas R. Powell, "Development in Early Literacy Skills during the
   Pre-Kindergarten Year in Head Start: Relations between Growth in
   Children's Writing and Understanding of Letters," *Early Childhood
   Research Quarterly* 23, no. 4 (2008): 467–78.
6. Marilyn J. Adams, *Beginning to Read: Thinking and Learning about Print*
   (Cambridge, MA: MIT Press, 1990), 108–115; Rebecca Treiman, Brett
   Kessler, Kelly Boland, Hayley Clocksin, and Zhengdao Chen, "Statistical
   Learning and Spelling: Older Prephonological Spellers Produce More
   Wordlike Spellings Than Younger Prephonological Spellers," *Child
   Development*, in press.
7. Amy Claessens, Mimi Engle, and F. Chris Curran, "Academic Content,
   Student Learning, and the Persistence of Preschool Effects," *American
   Educational Research Journal* 51, no. 2 (2014): 403–34.

8. Carlos Valiente, Jodi Swanson, and Nancy Eisenberg, "Linking Students' Emotions and Academic Achievement: When and Why Emotions Matter," *Child Development Perspectives* 6, no. 2 (2012): 129–35.

9. James W. Pellegrino and Margaret L. Hilton, eds., *Education for Life and Work: Developing Transferrable Knowledge and Skills in the 21st Century* (Washington, DC: The National Academies Press, 2012).

Part III

1. Connie Juel, "Learning to Read and Write: A Longitudinal Study of 54 Children from First through Fourth Grade," *Journal of Educational Psychology* 80, no. 4 (1988): 437–47; Elana Greenfield Spira, Stacey Storch Bracken, and Janet E. Fischel, "Predicting Improvement from First Grade Reading Difficulties: The Effects of Oral Language, Emergent Literacy, and Behavioral Skills," *Developmental Psychology* 41, no.1 (2005): 225–34.

2. Stacey A. Storch and Grover J. Whitehurst, "Oral Language and Code-related Precursors to Reading: Evidence from a Longitudinal Structural Model," *Developmental Psychology* 38, no. 6 (2002): 934–47; Valerie Muter, Charles Hulme, Margaret Snowling, and Jim Stevenson, "Phonemes, Rimes, Vocabulary, and Grammatical Skills as Foundations of Early Reading Development: Evidence from a Longitudinal Study," *Developmental Psychology* 40, no. 5 (2004): 665–81; Timothy Shanahan, "Thinking with Research: Research Changes Its Mind (Again)," *The Reading Teacher* 70, no. 2 (2016): 245–48; Jeanne R. Paratore, Christina M. Cassano, and Judith A. Schickedanz, "Supporting Early (and Later) Literacy Development at Home and at School," in *Handbook of Reading Research*, vol. IV, eds., Michael L. Kamil, P. David Pearson, Elizabeth Birr Moje, and Peter P. Afflerbach (New York: Routledge, 2011), 107–35.

Chapter 9

1. Jerome Bruner, *In Search of Mind: Essays in Biography* (New York: Harper & Row, Publishers, 1983), 183.

2. Marilyn J. Adams, *Beginning to Read* (Cambridge, MA: MIT Press, 1990), 108–15.

3. Sue Bredekamp, ed., *Developmentally Appropriate Practice in Early Childhood Programs Serving Children from Birth through Age 8* (Washington, DC: NAEYC, 1987); Sue Bredekamp and Carol Copple, eds., *Developmentally Appropriate Practice in Early Childhood Programs*, rev. ed. (Washington, DC: NAEYC, 1997); Susan B. Neuman, Carol Copple, and Sue Bredekamp, eds., *Learning to Read and Write: Developmentally Appropriate Practices for Young Children* (Washington, DC: NAEYC, 2000).

4. Judith A. Schickedanz, *More Than the ABCs* (Washington, DC: NAEYC, 1986); Judith A. Schickedanz, *Much More than the ABCs* (Washington, DC: NAEYC, 1999), 146–47; Judith A. Schickedanz and Molly F. Collins, *So Much More than the ABCs* (Washington, DC: NAEYC, 2013), 91–115.

5. Paul C. Quinn, Peter D. Eimas, and Stacey L. Rosenkrantz, "Evidence for Representation of Perceptually Similar Natural Categories by 3-Month-Old and 4-Month-Old Infants," *Perception* 23, no. 4 (1993): 463–75.

6. Eleanor Gibson, "Theory-based Research on Reading and Its Implications for Instruction," in *Toward a Literate Society*, eds., John B. Carroll and Jeanne S. Chall (New York: McGraw-Hill, 1975), 288–321.

7. Cynthia S. Puranik, Christopher J. Lonigan, and Young-Suk Kim, "Contributions of Emergent Literacy Skills to Name Writing, Letter Writing, and Spelling in Preschool Children," *Early Childhood Research Quarterly* 26, no. 4. (2011): 465–73.

8. National Association for Elementary School Principals, *Leading Pre-K-3 Learning Communities: Competencies for Effective Principal Practice* (Alexandria, VA: Author, 2014).

9. Victoria Purcell-Gates, "Stories, Coupons, and the 'TV Guide': Relationships between Home Literacy Experiences and Emergent Literacy Knowledge," *Reading Research Quarterly* 31, no. 4 (1996): 406–28; Amy Claessens, Mimi Engel, and F. Chris Curran, "Academic Content, Student Learning, and the Persistence of Preschool Effects," *American Educational Research Journal* 51, no. 2 (2014): 403–34.

Chapter 10

1. Charles Read, *Children's Categorization of Speech Sounds in English* (Urbana, IL: The National Council of Teachers of English, 1975) 36–39.

2. Carol S. Dweck, *Mindset* (New York: Ballantine Book, 2006); Carol S. Dweck, "The Perils and Promises of Praise," *Educational Leadership* 65, no. 2 (2007): 34–39.

3. Theodor A. Geisel, *Dr. Seuss's ABC* (New York: Random House, 1963).

4. Rebecca Treiman, Ruth Tincoff, Kira Rodriguez, and Angeliki Mouzaki et al., "The Foundations of Literacy: Learning the Sounds of Letters," *Child Development* 69, no. 6 (1998): 1524–40.

5. Jeffrey Elman, Elizabeth Bates, Mark H. Johnson, and Annette Karmiloff-Smith et al., *Rethinking Innateness* (Cambridge, MA: MIT Press, 1998), 130–47.

6. Allan Collins. John Seely Brown, and Ann Holum, "Cognitive Apprenticeship: Making Thinking Visible," *American Educator* 6, no.11 (1991): 38–46; Victoria Purcell-Gates, "Stories, Coupons, and the 'TV Guide': Relationships between Home Literacy Experiences and Emergent Literacy Knowledge," *Reading Research Quarterly* 31, no. 4 (1996): 406–28.

7. Geisel, *Dr. Seuss's ABC*, 12.

8. Frances D. Horowitz, "Child Development and the PITS: Simple Questions, Complex Answers, and Developmental Theory," *Child Development* 71, no.1 (2000): 5–6.

9. Judith A. Schickedanz and Molly F. Collins, *So Much More than the ABCs: The Early Phases of Reading and Writing* (Washington, DC: NAEYC, 2013).

10. Marilyn J. Adams, *Beginning to Read* (Cambridge, MA: MIT Press, 1990), 108–115; Rebecca Treiman, Brian Kessler, Kelly Boland, Hayley Clocksin, and Zhengdao Chen, "Statistical Learning and Spelling: Older Prephonlogical Spellers Produce More Wordlike Spellings Than Younger Prephonological Spellers," *Child Development*, in press.

11. Charles Read and Rebecca Treiman, "Children's Invented Spelling: What We Have Learned in Forty Years," in *Rich Languages from Poor Inputs*, eds., Masimmo Piattelli-Palmarini and Robert C. Berwick (New York: Oxford University Press, 2013), 197–211.

12. Massachusetts Department of Education, *Guidelines for Preschool Early Learning Standards* (Malden, MA: Author, 2003), 9–10.

13. Ingvar Lundberg, Jørgen Frost, and Ole-Peter Peterson, "Effects of an Extensive Program for Stimulating Phonological Awareness in Preschool Children," *Reading Research Quarterly* 23, no. 3 (1988): 263–84.

14. Jason L. Anthony, Christopher J. Lonigan, Kimberly Driscoll, and Beth Phillips et al., "Phonological Sensitivity: A Quasi-Parallel Progression of Word Structure Units and Cognitive Operations," *Reading Research Quarterly* 38, no. 4 (2003): 470–71; Teresa Ukrainetz, Janae J. Nuspl, Kimberly Wilkerson, and Sara R. Beddes, "The Effects of Syllable Instruction on Phonemic Awareness in Preschoolers," *Early Childhood Research Quarterly* 26, no.1 (2011): 50–60.

15. Purcell-Gates (1991), "Stories, Coupons, and the 'TV Guide'."

Chapter 11

1. Kathy Hirsh-Pasek and Roberta Michnick Golinkoff, *Celebrating the Scribble: Appreciating Children's Art* (Bethlehem, PA: Crayola Beginnings Press, 2007), 37.

2. David K. Dickinson, "Large Group and Free-Play Times: Conversational Settings Supporting Language and Literacy Development," in *Beginning Literacy with Language*, eds., David K. Dickinson and Patton O. Tabors (Baltimore, MD: Brookes, 2001), 223–55.

3. Elizabeth Meins, Charles Fernyhough, Rachel Wainwright, and Mani Das Gupta et al., "Maternal Mind-Mindedness and Attachment Security As Predictors of Theory of Mind Understanding," *Child Development* 73, no. 6 (2002): 1715–26.

4. Andrew J. Mashburn, Robert C. Pianta, Bridget K. Hamre, and Jason T. Downer et al., "Measures of Classroom Quality in Prekindergarten and Children's Development of Academic, Language, and Social Skills," *Child Development* 79, no. 3 (2008): 732–49.

5. Bridget Hatfield and Amanda P. Williford, "Cortisol Patterns for Young Children Displaying Disruptive Behavior: Links to a Teacher-Child Relationship-Focused Intervention," *Prevention Science* 18, no.1 (2017): 40–49.

6. Verna Aardema and Beatriz Vidal, illustrator, *Bringing the Rain to Kapiti Plain* (New York: Puffin Books, 1992), 20.

Chapter 12

1. Hazel Hutchins and Susan K. Hartung, illustrator, *One Dark Night* (New York: Viking Books, 2001).

2. J. Whitehurst Grover, David S. Arnold, Jeffrey N. Epstein, Andrea L. Angell, Meagan Smith, and Janet E. Fischel, "A Picture-Book Reading Intervention for Day Care and Home for Children from Low-Income Families," *Developmental Psychology* 30, no. 5 (1994): 679–89.

3. Pearson Early Learning, "Parent Notes for Reading *Hooray a Pinata!* by Elisa Kleven," in *Read Together, Talk Together Program* (Lebanon, IN: Pearson Learning, imprint of Pearson Education, 2006).

4. Ezra Jack Keats, *Peter's Chair* (New York: Puffin Books, 1967), 9–10.

5. Isabel Beck and Margaret McKeown, "Text Talk: Capturing the Benefits of Read-Aloud Experiences for Young Children," *The Reading Teacher* 55, no. 1 (2001): 12.

6. Christopher J. Lonigan, Jason L. Anthony, Brenlee G. Bloomfield, Sarah M. Dyer, and Corine S. Samwel, "Effects of Two Shared-Reading Interventions on Emergent Literacy Skills of At-Risk Preschoolers," *Journal of Early Intervention* 22, no. 4 (1999): 306–22.

7. Anne van Kleeck, "Providing Preschool Foundations for Later Reading Comprehension: The Importance of and Ideas for Targeting Inferencing in Storybook-Sharing Interventions," *Psychology in the Schools* 45, no. 7 (2008): 627–43; Elena Florit, Maja Roch, and M. Chiara Levorato, "Listening Text Comprehension in Preschoolers: A Longitudinal Study on the Role of Semantic Components," *Reading and Writing* 27, no. 5 (2014): 793–817.

8. Nell Duke and Joanne Carlisle, "The Development of Comprehension," in *Handbook of Reading Research*, vol. IV, eds., Michael L. Kamil, P. David Pearson, Elizabeth Birr Moye, and Peter P. Afflerbach (New York: Routledge, 2011), 199–228.

9. Lea M. McGee and Judith A. Schickedanz, "Repeated Interactive Read-Alouds in Preschool and Kindergarten," *The Reading Teacher* 60, no. 8 (2007): 742–51; Marilyn Cochran-Smith, *The Making of a Reader* (Norwood, NJ: Ablex, 1984).

10. David B. Yaden, "Parent-Child Storybook Reading As a Complex Adaptive System: Or 'An igloo is a house for bears,'" in *On Reading Books to Children*, eds., Anne van Kleeck, Stephen A. Stahl, and Eurydice B. Bauer (Mahwah, NJ: Lawrence Erlbaum, 2003), 336–62.

11. Judith A. Schickedanz and Molly F. Collins, "For Young Children, Pictures in Storybooks Are Rarely Worth a Thousand Words," *The Reading Teacher* 65, no. 8 (2012): 539–49.

12. Ana Carolina Brandao and Jane Oakhill, "How Do You Know This Answer?" Children's Use of Text Data and General Knowledge in Story Comprehension," *Reading and Writing* 18, nos.7–9 (2005): 687–713.

13. Elaine H. Hochenberger, Howard Goldstein, and Linda Sirianni Haas, "Effects of Commenting During Joint Book Reading by Mothers with Low SES," *Topics in Early Childhood Special Education* 19, no. 1(1999): 15–27; Jodi G. Fender and Kevin Crowley, "How Parent Explanation Changes What Children Learn from Everyday Scientific Thinking," *Journal of Applied Developmental Psychology* 28, no. 3 (2007): 189–210.

14. van Kleeck, "Providing Preschool Foundations for Later Reading Comprehension."

Part IV

1. Lee S. Shulman, "Those Who Understand Knowledge Growth in Teaching," *Educational Researcher* 15, no. 2 (1986): 9.

Chapter 13

1. Ezra Jack Keats, *The Snowy Day* (New York: Puffin Books, 1962).

2. Marie Ets, *Gilberto and the Wind* (New York: Puffin Books, 1979).

3. Ezra Jack Keats, *Whistle for Willie* (New York: Puffin Books, 1977).

4. Robert C. Pianta, Karen M. LaParo, and Bridget K. Hamre, *Classroom Assessment Scoring System, PreK Manual* (Baltimore, MD: Paul H. Brookes, 2008).

5. C. M. Mills, "Knowing When to Doubt: Developing a Critical Stance When Learning from Others," *Developmental Psychology* 49, no. 3 (2013): 404–18; Paul Harris, *Trusting What You're Told: How Children Learn from Others* (Cambridge, MA: Harvard University Press, 2012).

6. Robert McCloskey, *Make Way for Ducklings* (New York: Puffin Books, 1999).

7. Ruth Heller, *Chickens Aren't the Only Ones* (New York: Puffin Books, 1999).

8. Jim Arnosky, *Rabbits & Raindrops* (New York: Puffin Books, 2001).

9. Hazel Hutchins and Susan K. Hartung, illustrator, *One Dark Night* (New York: Viking Books, 2001).

10. Rosemary Wells, *Noisy Nora* (New York: Puffin Books, 2000).

11. Henry H. Wellman and Kristin H. Lagattuta, "Theory of Mind for Learning and Teaching: The Nature and Role of Explanation," *Cognitive Development* 19, no. 4 (2004): 479–97.

12. Don Freeman, *Corduroy* (New York: Puffin Books, 1976), 20.

13. Robert E. Haskell, *Transfer of Learning* (New York: Academic Press, 2001), 155–56.

14. Judith A. Schickedanz, "Increasing Children's Learning by Getting to the Bottom of Their Confusion," in *Achieving Excellence in Preschool Literacy Instruction*, eds., Laura M. Justice and Carol Vukelich (New York: Guilford, 2009), 182–97; Judith A. Schickedanz and Molly F. Collins, "For Young Children, Pictures in Storybooks Are Rarely Worth a Thousand Words," *The Reading Teacher* 65, no. 8 (2012): 539–49.

15. Elaine H. Hochenberger, Howard Goldstein, and Linda Sirianni Haas, "Effects of Commenting During Joint Book Reading by Mothers with Low SES," *Topics in Early Childhood Special Education* 19, no. 1(1999): 15–27; Jodi G. Fender and Kevin Crowley, "How Parent Explanation Changes What Children Learn from Everyday Scientific Thinking," *Journal of Applied Developmental Psychology* 28 no. 3 (2007): 189–210; Megan R. Luce, Maureen A. Callanan, and Sarah Smilovic, "Links between Parents' Epistemological Stance and Children's Evidence Talk," *Developmental Psychology* 49, no. 3 (2013): 454–61.

16. Pianta et al., *Classroom Assessment Scoring System, PreK Manual*.

17. Dale C. Farran, "We Need More Evidence in Order to Create Effective PreK Programs," *Economic Studies at Brookings, Evidence Speaks Reports* 1, no. 11 (2016): 4.

Chapter 14

1. Allan Collins, John Seely Brown, and Susan E. Newman, "Cognitive Apprenticeship: Making Thinking Visible" (Urbana: University of Illinois, Center for the Study of Reading, 1987).

2. Theodor S. Geisel, *Dr. Seuss's ABC* (New York: Random House, 1963).

3. Bill Martin, John Archambault, and Lois Ehlert, illustrator, *Chicka Chicka Boom Boom* (New York: Beach Lane Books, 2000).

Chapter 15

1. Mary Azarian, *The Gardener's Alphabet* (Boston: Houghton-Mifflin, 2000).
2. Charles Read, *Children's Categorization of Speech Sounds in English* (Urbana, IL: National Council of Teachers of English, 1975).
3. Marie M. Clay, *Writing Begins at Home* (Auckland, New Zealand: Heinemann Educational Books, 1987); Linda O. Lavine, "Differentiation of Letterlike Forms in Prereading Children," *Developmental Psychology* 13, no. 2 (1977): 89–94.
4. J. Richard Gentry, "A Retrospective on Invented Spelling and a Look Forward," *The Reading Teacher* 54, no. 3 (2000): 318–32; Gene Ouellette and Monique Senechal, "Pathways to Literacy: A Study of Invented Spelling and Its Role in Learning to Read," *Child Development* 79, no. 4 (2008): 899–913; Gene Ouellette and Monique Senechal, "Invented Spelling in Kindergarten as a Predictor of Reading and Spelling in Grade 1: A New Pathway to Literacy, or Just the Same Road, Less Known?," *Developmental Psychology* 53, no. 1 (2017): 77–88; Donald Richgels, "Invented Spelling Ability and Printed Word Learning in Kindergarten," *Reading Research Quarterly* 30, no.1 (1995): 96–109.
5. Rebecca Treiman, Brett Kessler, Kelly Boland, Hayley Clocksin, and Zhengdao Chen, "Statistical Learning and Spelling: Older Prephonological Spellers Produce More Wordlike Spellings than Younger Prephonological Spellers," *Child Development*, in press.

Chapter 16

1. Connie Juel, "Learning to Read and Write: A Longitudinal Study of Children From First Through Fourth Grades," *Journal of Educational Psychology* 80, no. 4 (1988): 437–47; Elana Greenfield Spira, Stacey Storch Bracken, and Janet E. Fischel, "Predicting Improvement After First Grade Reading Difficulties: The Effects of Oral Language, Emergent Literacy, and Behavior Skills," *Developmental Psychology* 41, no.1 (2005): 225–34.
2. Greg Duncan et al., "School Readiness and Later Achievement," *Developmental Psychology* 43, no. 6 (2007): 1428–46.
3. Sue Bredekamp, ed., *Developmentally Appropriate Practice in Early Childhood*

Programs Serving Children from Birth to Age 8 (Washington, DC: NAEYC, 1987); Sue Bredekamp and Carol Copple, eds., *Developmentally Appropriate Practice in Early Childhood Programs*, rev. ed. (Washington, DC: NAEYC, 1997); Carol Copple and Sue Bredekamp, eds., *Developmentally Appropriate Practice in Early Childhood Programs Serving Children from Birth through Age 8*, 3rd ed. (Washington, DC: NAEYC, 2009), 1–31.

4. Susan B. Neuman, Carol Copple, and Sue Bredekamp, eds., *Learning to Read and Write: Developmentally Appropriate Practice for Young Children* (Washington, DC: NAEYC, 2000); National Association for the Education of Young Children (NAEYC) and the National Council of the Teachers of Mathematics (NCTM), *Early Childhood Mathematics: Promoting Good Beginnings* (Washington, DC: NAEYC, 2002), 1–21.

5. Robert C. Pianta, Karen M. LaParo, and Bridget K. Hamre, *The Classroom Assessment Scoring System CLASS* (Baltimore: Paul H. Brookes, 2008).

6. David Dickinson, "Book Reading in Preschool Classrooms: Is Recommended Practice Common?" in *Beginning Literacy with Language*, eds., David Dickinson and Patton O. Tabors (Baltimore: Paul H. Brookes, 2001), 175–203.

7. William H. Teale, Melanie Walski, Emily Hoffman, Maureen Meeham, Colleen Whittingham, and Anna Colaner, *Early Childhood Literacy: Policy for the Coming Decade*, Policy Brief 4, no. 1 (Chicago: UIC Research on Urban Education Policy Initiative, 2016).

8. *Common Core State Standards for English Language Arts and Literacy in History/Social Studies, Science and Technical Subjects*, www.corestandards. org/assets/CCSSI_ELA%20Standards.pdf; *Next Generation Science Standards*, www.nextgenscience.org.

Chapter 17

1. Kenneth Leithwood, Karen Seashore Louis, Stephen Anderson, and Kyla Wahlstrom, *How Leadership Influences Student Learning* (New York: The Wallace Foundation, 2004), 5; Linda Darling-Hammond, Ruth Chung Wei, Alethea Andree, and Nikole Richardson et al., *Professional Learning in the Learning Profession: A Status Report on Teacher Development in the United States and Abroad* (Dallas, TX: National Staff Development Council, 2009).

2. Heather J. Lavigne, Karen Shakman, Jacqueline Zweig, and Sara L. Greller, *Principals' Time, Tasks, and Professional Development: An Analysis of Schools and Staffing Survey Data* (Waltham, MA: REL Northeast and Islands at EDC, 2016), 13.

3. Kwang Suk Yoon, Teresa Duncan, Silvia Wen-Yu Lee, and Beth Scarloss et al., *Reviewing the Evidence on How Teacher Professional Development Affects Student Achievement* (Austin, TX: REL Southwest, 2007), 1–5; Allison Gulamhussein, *Effective Professional Development in an Era of High Stakes Accountability* (Alexandria, VA: The Center for Public Education, 2013), 3–18.

4. Tim Waters and Greg Cameron, *The Balanced Leadership Framework: Connecting Vision with Action* (Denver, CO: McREL, 2007), 27–30.

5. William H. Teale, Melanie Walski, Emily Hoffman, Maureen Meehan, Colleen Whittingham, and Anna Colaner, "Early Childhood Literacy: Policy for the Coming Decade," *Policy Brief* 4, no. 1 (Chicago: UIC Center for Research on Urban Education Policy Initiative, 2016).

6. Thomas R. Gusky and Kwang Suk Yoon, "What Works in Professional Development?," *Phi Delta Kappan* 90 no. 7 (2009): 495–500; Bradley A. Ermeling and Jessica Yarbo, "Expanding Instructional Horizons: A Case Study of Teacher Team-Outside Expert Partnerships," *Teachers College Record* 118, no. 2 (2016): 1–48.

7. *Teaching the Teachers: At a Glance* (Alexandria, VA: Center for Public Education, 2013); Darling-Hammond et al., *Professional Learning in the Learning Profession.*

8. Jana Hunzicker, *Characteristics of Effective Professional Development: A Checklist* (Peoria, IL: Bradley University, 2010), 7–8, retrieved from ERIC database Number ED510366.

9. Kenneth Leithwood et al., *Review of Research: How Leadership Influences Student Learning* (New York: The Wallace Foundation, 2004), 27–29.

10. Phyllis H. Lindstrom and Marsha Speck, *The Principal as Professional Development Leader* (Thousand Oaks, CA: Corwin Press, 2004).

11. Anne Lewis, *Revisioning Professional Development: What Learner Centered Professional Development Looks Like* (Oxford, OH: National Staff Development Council, 1999).

Chapter 18

1. Timothy Shanahan and Christopher J. Lonigan, "The National Early Literacy Panel: A Summary of the Process and the Report," *Educational Researcher* 39, no. 4 (2010): 279–85; Judith A. Schickedanz and Molly F. Collins, *So Much More Than the ABCs: The Early Phases of Reading and Writing* (Washington, DC: NAEYC, 2013), 91–126.

2. Eileen M. O'Brien and Chuck Dervarics, *Pre-kindergarten: What the Research Shows* (Alexandria, VA: Center for Public Education, 2007); Deborah A. Phillips et al., "Puzzling It Out: The Current State of Scientific Knowledge on Pre-Kindergarten Effects," in *The Current State of Scientific Knowledge on Pre-Kindergarten Effects* (Washington, DC: Brookings Institution, 2017), 19–29.

3. Ann S. Epstein, *The Intentional Teacher: Choosing the Best Strategies for Young Children's Learning*, rev. ed. (Washington, DC: NAEYC, 2015); Deena Skolnick Weisberg et al., "Making Play Work for Education," *Phi Delta Kappan* 96, no. 8 (2015): 8–13.

4. James W. Pellegrino and Margaret L. Hilton, eds., *Education for Life and Work: Developing Transferrable Knowledge and Skills in the 21st Century* (Washington, DC: The National Academies Press, 2012), 1–14.

5. Schickedanz and Collins, *So Much More Than the ABCs: The Early Phases of Reading and Writing*, 7–17.

6. John Payton et al., *The Positive Impact of Social and Emotional Learning for Kindergarten to Eighth-Grade Students: Findings from Three Scientific Reviews* (Chicago: Collaborative for Academic, Social, and Emotional Learning, 2008).

ACKNOWLEDGMENTS

WITH ALMOST FIFTY YEARS APIECE AS TEACHERS of young children and their teachers, we owe large debts of gratitude to many people for welcoming us into their schools and classrooms. These people include principals, early childhood directors, content-area specialists, coaches and mentors, and, most of all, teachers. All shared their ideas and concerns about children and teaching, and also listened to ours. The willingness of teachers to try things and provide feedback, and to invite us to see for ourselves by working directly with their children, provided ideal opportunities for both of us to learn. Our decision to use classroom events, developed into cases, puts both children and teachers front and center, in ways we hope do justice to both. All chapters are based on real situations we observed or experienced as participants, though most also are a composite of more than one experience, because we often broadened the key event in each chapter by including information from closely related events that occurred in other classrooms. In this way, we could make each chapter as rich and informative as possible, and increase the likelihood that readers can see themselves in it.

This book involved a kind of writing that was new to both of us, more akin to storytelling than typical expository presentation. At first, when thinking about our experiences with teachers and children, we relived each one to the fullest and included too many details in its retelling. Our wonderfully supportive and patient editor Nancy Walser kept suggesting "not to get so deeply into the weeds" that a reader can't see the big ideas. "Weeds," in this case, were actually good plants that we had placed where they cast shadows on more important ideas for a chapter. With her help, we gradually worked our way out of the weeds to more focused, yet still rich, chapters. Our thanks, as well, to Sumita Mukherji for her terrific support during the production phases.

We must also mention the support of our spouses, including their patience in tolerating violations of the expectation that, in retirement, we would have more time to travel, visit with and talk about grandchildren, and linger over dinner. Thanks for hanging in there, David and Edward!

ABOUT THE AUTHORS

Judith A. Schickedanz, a professor emerita at Boston University, is a leading expert in early childhood education and early literacy. At BU, she founded the laboratory preschool (and served as director for eighteen years), served as BU's early childhood consultant to the Boston University and the Chelsea Public Schools collaborative, and taught both undergraduate and graduate courses in child development, early education, and early literacy. She has extensive experience in creating preschool curriculum and working with teachers and school leaders in Chelsea (1990–1993); Boston (1976–1981, funding from a Right-to-Read Grant, US DOE); and many Early Reading First projects across the country (2003–2012, funding from No Child Left Behind to create "centers of excellence" in preschool education).

Schickedanz served on the committee to update accreditation standards for NAEYC and as president of the Literacy Development in Young Children SIG within IRA (now ILA). She has published many articles, book chapters, and books. Her books include *Strategies for Teaching Young Children* (1977, 1983, 1990, with M. York, I. Stewart, and D. White); *So Much More than the ABCs* (2013, with M. Collins; earlier editions authored solely, 1986 and 1999); *Curriculum in Early Childhood: A Resource Guide for Kindergarten and Preschool Teachers* (1997, with M. Pergantis, J. Kanosky, and J. Ottinger); *Writing in Preschool: Orchestrating Meaning and Marks* (2004; 2009, with R. Casbergue); *Increasing the Power of Instruction; Integration of Language, Literacy, and Math across the Preschool Day* (2008); and *Adam's Righting Revolutions* (1990). She is the senior author of a preschool curriculum, *Opening the World of Learning* (2005, with D. Dickinson). She was also the senior author of four editions of *Understanding Children and Adolescents*, a child development text.

Catherine Marchant, EdD, has been a classroom teacher, a teacher educator, an instructional coach and an administrator (e.g., early childhood liaison, evaluation team leader, and early childhood specialist). She began her career as early childhood special educator in the Boston Public Schools. At Wheelock College (1982–1994), she taught courses in children's development and curriculum and instruction and also supervised student teachers. Later, she served as a literacy coach in Boston's early education centers, and then as an instructional coach for the Boston Early Reading First initiative, in collaboration with Judy Schickedanz, the curriculum consultant. Catherine has also served as an early childhood coach and professional development provider for BPS Department of Early Childhood.

Currently, Catherine consults with individual schools and districts helping them develop curriculum based on the principles and examples provided in *Opening the World of Learning* (OWL, 2005) and providing professional development in which she shares both hands-on experiences obtained in work with a wide range of children and teachers, and relevant research and theory. Catherine holds three degrees in education: a bachelor's from Boston College, a master's from Teachers College, Columbia University, and a doctorate from the Harvard Graduate School of Education.

INDEX